With A Twist

Your Cocktail Personality Guide to Finding Love & Romance

Straight Up With A Twist: Your Cocktail Personality Guide to
Finding Love & Romance

Straight Up With A Twist: Your Cocktail Personality Guide to
Finding Love & Romance

This publication is designed to provide information in regard to the
subject matter covered. In so doing, neither the publisher nor the
author is engaged in rendering legal, accounting, or other
professional services. If you require legal advice or other expert
assistance, you should seek the services of a professional
specializing in the particular discipline required.

While the author has made every effort to provide accurate
information at the time of publication, neither the publisher nor the
author assumes any responsibility for errors, or for changes that
occur after publication.

FIRST EDITION
Photography and Cover Design by Heidi M. Gress

CONTENTS

DEDICATION

This book is for all the boys who served me up on a platter:

Bubble Boy, Opera Boy, Cruise Boy, Granola Boy 1&2, Trust Fund Boy, Litigator Boy, Charity Boy, Doctor Boy, Elevated Boy, The Down Under Wonder, Burning Man, Margin Call Man, Italian Stallion, Captain, Greek Guy, Rock of Ages, RCD, Bridge Man...

Without you, I might still be wandering aimlessly around the produce aisle of life instead of having my cake and eating it too! Thank you for showing me time and again how I showed up in your world, "shaken and stirred." Because of your dining habits and cocktail concoctions and after many luscious libations, I finally realized that I needed to examine my own inner mixology and create a recipe for my life that was fit for a queen! Today I live "Straight Up With A Twist" and can offer my insights into how to live your best life and find real love and long lasting romance to women worldwide who sadly find themselves swimming in the bottom of their champagne flutes instead of bubbling up to the top and becoming who they were born to be!

Chapter 1

WHY WOMEN DINE ALONE

Today, I ate lunch alone. Everywhere I looked, I saw women dining alone. It's an epidemic!

Take it from someone who relishes in lavish and not so lavish delectables and lingering libations. Being the only fork holder at the table gets old quickly. The guilt following the splurge keeps psychologists in business and diet clubs chomping at the bit. Reading these tea leaves does not require a mystic or a culinary king. The reason we fly solo at the buffet is quite simple: WE CHOOSE TO!

So girls, it's really about manifesting what you want. Stop hiding behind the saccharine sweet illusion of what shoulda, coulda, woulda been, if only I didn't have my mother's thighs, my father's eyes, and I hadn't been raised on the set of *The Taming of the Shrew*. Oh, wait. I *was* raised on that set, and the shrew is me! You see, becoming a fully actualized woman requires living naked. We must throw our cares to the wind, get a camera with an HD lens, and refuse to remain covered and insecurely positioned within the flawed fairy tales of our youth. "I have no prince. My horse is lame. I am upside down on the mortgage to my castle. There are so many knots in my hair that even Rapunzel would opt for a crew cut. The dwarfs make my life so freaking miserable, I should have been a nun."

You see, our own dastardly plots to be free have created our lives, our inner mixology, and our menus. We have become indulgent, entitled, and remain totally in denial. So let's move out beyond the prison of delusion and try independence and self-satisfaction for a change. Fulfillment starts with being responsible for oneself— physically, emotionally, intellectually, financially, sexually, socially, and spiritually. We can only choose a Straight Up With A Twist life after we truly find ourselves worth the price of our cocktail creation.

How do we learn to say, "I am a top-shelf woman" and mean it? We must first admit that we have cooked this lifestyle up ourselves! Yes, we learned how to "bring home the bacon and fry it up in the pan" in the early 70s and have been eating TV dinners ever since. Our self-image slipped away with our grandmother's recipes. Thirty years later, our dreams of wearing stilettos by night and a Superwoman T-shirt by day has made a fortune for the pharmaceutical industry but hasn't worked out that well for most of us. Our life goals of independence, career success, perfect children, and a soul mate became gelatin instead of mousse. Eventually we started to believe that gaining five pounds a year, enduring hot flashes, depression, and serial monogamy were the natural order of life. Sisters, those annual pounds are not natural. They are a consequence of filling up our emptiness with food that never makes us truly satiated. No amount of ice cream, chocolate, or Chardonnay can make us feel full or happy. A Straight Up With A Twist Girl says, "I accept who I am— a delicious, perfect, divine soul having a unique and totally human experience. My life and the communion that I offer others and myself are not simply a piece of me but the whole of me. I am enough for me. I am full and present and conscious. I choose my life, my menu, and my pairings."

Yes, living in the present and satisfying ourselves may appear incredibly selfish and narcissistic. Surely many people rest in the egocentric aspects of their personas forever. At a closer look, however, their meals are missing several courses. There is a difference between narcissism and actualization. Narcissism mutually excludes any other diner; actualization is totally inclusive, a sumptuous buffet. Narcissism describes a person who only exists as a reflection—their reality is created by the number of stars they receive in their restaurant review. They're looking good but have no flavor. When the lights are out and the restaurant is empty, they are consumed by loneliness. They are prisoners of the façade they create. A narcissist is all shallow essence and spicy additives. There is no real meat. No one else exists in his or her life except the current patrons. Their revolving love interests live with a mirror in one hand and glass cleaner in their back pocket.

Living fully conscious and actualized means that a person chooses to live "in the loving." The first choice is to love ourselves. Once we truly love ourselves and satisfy our own needs, we are free to choose to love another, or many others, freely—without boundaries and without fear. No one can threaten our identity. We can be hurt, but if we remain constant in the loving, the pain will become compassionate caring, as we experience the other as love. We can choose to love without expecting anything in return. Wow, what a concept!

So how does this play out in real life? First, we must be prepared to give up our diet of pabulum and neurotic self-manipulation and choose honesty. Easier said than done.

So how does this look, this new divine order?

It is a place where men and women are divinely different and yet gorgeously compatible in celebrating the buffet of life. How do we survive in the backlash of the feminist cannibalism and the male malaise?

It came to me the other day. I was hearing the violins tuning up for another hypnotic rendition of "Am I Blue?" The heart-piercing soliloquy rang in my ears as I watched another commitment-phobic, divorced, damaged, fifty-eight-year-old man sail me out to sea because I was so "perfect." My mother's voice came streaming through in high def sound. "If you're giving the milk away for free, why should he buy the cow?" Meanwhile, the Greek chorus was chanting, "F*** him if he can't take a joke!" I realized that I was...all of a sudden, everything began to spin.

The silent alto chant of my inner counselor gently but firmly bellowed, "The whole paradigm is wrong, Mary. Remember when you lived in your own paradigm of loving? Reclaim it. Create a new hybrid for relationships. Start with creating your own menu." I did. I eat what I want, when I want; I pay the bill and retire satisfied. Every meal offers so many choices. My glass is always half full, not half empty, and I never clean my plate.

Maybe the failure to love is simply defaulting to fear. If there are only two motivators in life—love and fear—we have

8

definitely plunged headfirst into fear, otherwise known as the prix fixe love menu. Our five course choices are made for us. We may not be crazy about all the offerings, but at least the dessert looks promising. One thing is for sure: we will not starve. And what a bargain. We know the price we are paying for our meal. We settle for less. We will be hungry again in a few hours. We embrace linear loving like we line up for an all-you-can-eat buffet. It's what we've been taught. The feminist manifesto destroyed most of our taste buds along with manipulating our inner sanctum of self-respect and true love. The paradigm is broken. Women barter. Men barter. We compete for market share. We do battle. We overeat. We all lose. We do not love. We arbitrate and stuff ourselves. We make deals. We do not trust. We do not love. We live in fear. We occasionally step on the scales of integrity and lie to ourselves about our diet. We are the enemy. Instead of crying in our soup, we need to create an entire new recipe for a relationship. We need to eat dessert first and bake a cake using ingredients that are fresh and real and taste good. Let's start with authenticity.

Let us first examine and accept the obvious:
Ladies,

WE ARE ALL BY OURSELVES. WE DINE AND
SLEEP ALONE!

Chapter 2

ALL ABOUT EVE: THE APPLE DID US IN!

From the very beginning of time, a disconnect has existed between the sexes. Eve was interested in eating the apple and not so secretly seduced Adam into taking a bite, and look what happened. Adam just wanted to eat Eve. If Eve had abandoned her insecurity and controlling nature, she would have just eaten Adam.

Adam would have eaten Eve. They would have made passionate, unbridled love, pranced through the garden, and grabbed a bite later—a piece of ass, and a sip of divine nectar...a Good Humor bar. But no, she had to distract Adam from his goal. She put a lock on herself. She substituted her libido, longing for a frigging piece of fruit. And they both were damned to Hell for eternity.

GREAT! Talk about original sin. Welcome to life as we know it. Relationships have rarely worked since—all for a lousy apple and a turn holding the reins. I rest my case.

From the beginning of time, man and woman have been divinely made in a mutually exclusive fashion. The very DNA structure provides us with a direct focus on fulfilling our needs, most often at the cost of our desires. Since we are unwilling to accept the reality of our irreconcilable differences and constantly use an archaic method of manipulation and miscommunication to measure our merit, feather our beds, and tickle our fancy, we continue to lose market share. What does this mean? If you don't like the cocktail, change the recipe.

Men want to have their way with us. We want a man to love us. The procreation part is fabulous; the love forever after sucks. Men lie because it's easier than confrontation. Women manipulate and use sex as a tool for getting what they think they want. Both become dissatisfied, disillusioned, depressed, and done. Women stock the fridge. Men discover the babe buffet. Women gain weight and commiserate with their miserable friends at a youth enhancing party. Men live alone and delight in every piece of ass on the menu. Women go to a yoga retreat. Men join a dating site. Pure and simple, it just doesn't work.

Let me explain. When a man sees a woman he is attracted to, he wants to have sex with her. You know, ravage her body, delight in her loins, and then languish in the spoils of spreading his seed. When a woman sees a man she is attracted to, she begins to envision herself becoming every fairytale princess that ever lived—she wants to receive all-encompassing and everlasting love: swept away, worshipped and adorned, wined and dined, romanced, defended and possessed, betrothed and be true. She wants to be trapped in the trappings of her design and live happily ever after...and then maybe she'll have sex, eventually...and a blowjob on their wedding night. And that, my friends, is the beginning of the end.

Women somehow weigh love in assets, not in being a piece of ass. They have an unquenchable desire to acquire stuff, a sad substitute for security but a good front for feeling loved. Women want to be taken care of—you know, "kept in the style to which they have become accustomed."

Last time I looked, most of the women I know *never* were accustomed to what they think they deserve, and somehow they feel entitled to have that life and have it paid for by some poor schlep who just thinks they are cute and wants to take a closer look.

Ladies, if we take a real, un-retouched look at ourselves in the mirror without the aid of filters or drugs, we might see the sad truth.

We are insecure and getting older withevery breath. Somewhere we heard we were "special," and now we think we should be given a dowry more substantial than the assets of a small country.

In addition to this bequest, we think that after convincing some poor guy to work like a slave for the honor of spending eternity basking in our presence, we should no longer have to give him what he really wants: our body, our respect, and a hot meal once in a while. In addition to this bargain he's getting, we have become delusional enough to believe that we should be able to SAY, DO, BECOME, and LOOK like anything we want for the rest of our life, rule the roost, let ourselves go, and still maintain our place on the throne. Oh, and we now never have sex unless there's additional bling involved—and even then it's not the way it once was...accentuating the *once*. My God, are you kidding? Who is buying this crap? The only dessert your hardworking, sucker-punched man is eating, honey, is frozen. Boys, better watch that first bite—it's a bitch!

Okay, enough about Eve, and us. Let's talk about him.

The truth is this. Men are over it. They have taken the cure. Thanks to feminism, alimony, prenuptials, and the fact that their former wives became Martha in *Who's Afraid of Virginia Wolf*, he is aware of your charms and has the scars to prove it. His bank account and the fact that his kids no longer speak to him except to ask for money—and then refer to him as their "sperm donor"—has left him rather sphinxlike these days. The rules have changed, girls. Get over it. Get used to it. Stop crying. The skin never goes back, and for God's sake, stop eating!

Do you want to find your soul mate or not? If you do, start taking notes. If you don't, sayonara, have another mojito, and don't forget to ask for a doggy bag.

The only relationship that really matters is the one you have with yourself. Finding the partner of your dreams must begin with becoming the woman of your dreams first.

Makin' Bacon: Our Post-feminist Manifesto

I often wonder, "How did we get into this pathetic corner?" All we ever really wanted was to be happy in whatever form that was created. At some point, most of us really want to find one guy who has little or no baggage, or at least less than ours. We have dutifully become independent women, lest we be stoned by our feminist sisters.

We courageously became professionals, burned our bra, rallied behind our manifestos, and dove headfirst into the "make love, not war" coed dorm milieu. Some of our friends had "benefits," and some of our boyfriends had game, but all in all, we bought into being the guinea pigs for the women's lib movement. We have now realized most of us have been left holding the bag, even if it is a very pretty little luxury ditty that we paid for ourselves.

Many of us who tried to "have it all"—a career, marriage, children, and be a mother, daughter, lover, and wife—are now quite dissatisfied and depressed. We are finding ourselves exhausted, dazed, and alone. The men, who have become very confused by the battle of the sexes, have now realized that not only do they not have to commit or marry anyone, they don't even have to pay for the date! It makes a girl sick to her stomach. Most eligible men have no interest in settling down. Girls are ripe for the picking, and the rules have changed. Admittedly, most men after a certain age have been burned badly by an ex-wife and will never get taken advantage of again. They feel entitled to enjoy what time they have left. After all, their virility is waning, and those hotties will soon move on to greener pastures. They have their kids and half of their money, so why commit?

In addition to this startling revelation, it has occurred to me that my life has been a series of out-of-body experiences. My choices were really simple: either I continue to live the "*Father Knows Best*" paradigm and costar in my life, never living up to my own potential, or I could break free from those archaic restraints and become independent, creating a brand new paradigm for being female.

In theory, this choice had real potential for success. Unfortunately, an entire generation of women soon discovered that our emotional beings were not prepared for the future that our intellectual and physical beings aspired to manifest. We knew that we would cause a revolution, but we had no idea that the body count would be so high after winning the equality war. The rest of the world was forced to change along with us. Villages raised children, men took paternity leave, we paid alimony, and health statistics showed that heart disease was on the rise due to the stress caused by women living in the "real world." Perhaps our hearts were breaking as a result of the disillusionment we experienced once we grabbed the brass ring.

Many of us gained the world, but lost ourselves in the process. We began to live our entire lives in the default setting, making lemonade out of lemons instead of deciding what we wanted to drink. We got divorced, wound up as single moms, took care of our ailing parents, went back to school, took vacations with the girls, and cried ourselves to sleep with a chocolate chip cookie and a glass of Chardonnay. We were in a tailspin. We didn't want to take responsibility for being the creation of our problems or the salvation of our souls. The real question that I continually ask myself is: Why did I do this? Why do I keep making the same mistakes over and over again? Why am I alone?

My mother used to say, "Mary Susan, if someone told you to hold your hand to a hot stove, would you do it?" I did, over and over again, because it seemed appropriate at the time. I found myself applying a lot of burn cream. I was born to decorate other people's lives. I am excellent at it. I believed that if I were just perfect enough, someone would find me desirable enough to love. I did not feel that I deserved to be loved, because I didn't love myself. I was

15

afraid of the "big reveal." Mary is not enough! In addition to not feeling worthy of respect and happiness, I had no idea who I really was underneath the frills and precepts. I had no idea about what I wanted to be when I grew up, or even if I wanted to grow up. Once I took away all the layers of sauces and marinades, garnishes, and pretty serving dishes, I had no idea what to do with the raw ingredients of my being. I existed only as a menu offering to others and had no grasp on becoming the perfect pairing for myself.

Years later, my teenage daughter fired a heat-seeking missile at my heart: "Mom, when are you going to take the doormat sign off your forehead? I see the way you live your life and how that worked out. There is no way *I'm* letting anyone run my life, especially not some guy." She sadly hit the nail on the head. I never thought about preparing a meal for myself. As long as I spent my life making others happy, satisfied, and secure, I felt happy. My life depended upon my attention being other-centered, distracting me from ever discovering my own worth. If I was not busy preparing meals for someone else, I felt hollow and unwanted.

Even with all the success and beauty and accolades, I only felt fulfilled if someone else loved me and complimented my cooking. I only felt good enough if I could exist on the crumbs left on a table set for someone else's pleasure. And so, we continue makin' bacon, and usually dine alone.

Chapter 3

THE LADIES WHO LUNCH LIE

"Let's do lunch!" This innocent phrase provides the meal that is worth repeating. Get out your heartburn meds and prepare for a full-frontal examination of the lies we love to discuss over lunch. These secretly simple catchphrases have become the very fiber of our existence, and a consistent diet of ingesting these malicious morsels keeps us in the "bingeing and purging club," far from adopting a healthy diet of truth and lean protein.

You see, from birth we have been fed a diet of excuse-laden pabulum to protect our feelings and keep us from accepting responsibility and accountability regarding our life choices and menu descriptions. These little phrases become our mantras and maintain the myths we hold to be true. Don't believe me? Take a few nibbles and see if you've swallowed a few of them at your last female-friendly gathering. My bet is that the scales will tip in the direction of truth, and some of these lies have kept your palette perking since your very first birthday party.

1.   "IT'S NOT YOUR FAULT. IT'S ALL
     IN THE GENES!"

"How do you stay so thin? You must have good genes."

My entire life has been summarized and arbitrarily dismissed by this phrase. Honestly, ladies, the only good

17

genes I have are the ones I've been wearing for the past
five years, $9.99. And the only other inherited beneficial
genes attributed to my lean machine are the predisposed
DNA to be disciplined, energetic, and determined. Give me
a break. The rest of my looks can be attributed to years of
daily calorie counting, thousands of miles on the treadmill
(and other less forgiving surfaces) accompanied by years
of self-denial and countless smile lines earned from trying
to be polite when that mantra is sent in my direction by
overweight women sitting across from me, stuffing
themselves with a pulled pork sandwich, fries, and a Diet
Coke. Just accept the fact that I work my tail off to stay the
way I look. NO ONE GETS A FREE PASS!

This sort of blatant "magical thinking" and total lack of
accountability, culpability, ownership of your body, and
ability to keep your mouth shut will only send you further
down the road of "poor, poor, pitiful fat me!"

Ladies, good genes have very little to do with how we look.
The keys to the kingdom lie in taking in fewer calories than
we burn, day after day, year after year. Although genes
play a part in our overall body shape, our metabolic rate
can be increased and our appetites decreased once we
demystify the reason behind our emotional eating.

The payoff of believing "it's all in the genes" probably
started with your mother making excuses for your weight,
eye color, or some other perceived inadequacy in order to
protect you from the real world and yourself. In order to not
have your feelings hurt, she started to create an elaborate
diet of feeding you subtle lies about yourself and her that

would distract you from the truth about who you are. These lies were intended to protect your feelings and promote a healthy self-image. They were fabricated to remove certain obstacles in your life that you don't have "control over" in order to advance you in the areas where you have a natural gift. It's sort of like cheating.

Everyone who hears the excuse knows you're doing it, but no one wants to discuss it. Instead, they insulate your emotions by offering you a reason for your lack of self-control, distance you from knowing yourself and dealing with the feelings you are obviously stuffing down your throat. These lies prevent you from taking responsibility for who you are and misguide you by leading you into decisions that create unhealthy habits in self-care. These culturally accepted lies provide you with an excuse that creates a self-sabotaging defeatist attitude for your entire life. It's the meal that keeps on giving, an excuse for all seasons. If we do not have to take responsibility for our physiological, mental, and emotional being by attributing everything we do not like about ourselves to our gene pool and our ancestry, how are we ever going to discover our true potential and live happy, independent lives?

This is a lie straight from the fad diet of our lives: "eat all you want and still lose weight." No one is going to do our work for us. We are the only ones buying this bingeing lie. We are what we eat, and we will eat ourselves into oblivion if we do not accept responsibility for creating our own naked recipes for life. Every time we see someone who looks the way we would like to look, we devise a reason why we do not measure up. The excuse gets regurgitated and we continue to believe it. Trust me, I have been asked

19

a million times how I stay so thin and fit. I tell people that basically I have never spent a day in my life without keeping count of my calories, and I am never without the mental calculator navigating my day. Neurotic? Yes. Crazy? Yes. Worth it? For me, yes!

But as soon as I mention exercise, relentless calorie counting, and denial, women's eyes glass over, and then they give me that look of indignation and say, "Yeah, well, your mother was thin and beautiful. It's your genes!" Then they supersize their meal and we're off to the races.

If you elect to supersize, accept the fact that you're going to be fat and get over it. Inside every thin woman is a fat chick dying for a loaded pizza. We just need to say no—at least most of the time. Do your looks and weight affect your life? Yes! Have you ever met a Happy Hippo? Yes! What's the difference? Women who are buying the gene story and who actually make conscious choices about the value of food in their lives can accept the result of their choice. They have decided that what they eat is more important than how they look. Do they have issues? Don't we all?

2.   "HE HAS POTENTIAL."

He is a project, not a prospect.

Okay, we have all been there. This is code for "I am so desperate for a man, that I can eke out an attempt at ever after by wrapping my head around the fact that this loser is a work in progress." No, he is not. You are setting yourself up for an eventual upset tummy and a total waste of time.

This guy is not a prospect; he is a project. And for most women, it is much more palatable to perfect someone else's flaws and polish their rough edges than to work on changing our own flaws and chiseling our own coal into a brilliant diamond.

Projects display clear signs of their mental framework and foibles. Let's see how many you can check off:

A. "I just love a woman in uniform...a nurse's' uniform that is!"

Florence Nightingales of the world—LISTEN!! These guys find you because they can spot you a mile away, just like all the homeless people, crazies, and stray puppies and kittens. TURN OFF THE GPS! You manifest what you believe to be true about yourself. What is it in you that requires you to post "the doctor is in" sign outside your door and the "doormat" sign on your forehead? Do you need to be needed this much? Is the only way you think that you can have a relationship is if you become a martyr in the process? Self-esteem—are you in there somewhere??

B. "Enough about you. Let's talk about me."

He discloses his life story on the first date and seeks immediate triage. He takes off all his bandages and shows you all his scars and bruises in hopes that you can heal them.

C.   "She ain't heavy, she's my mother."

Most projects have or had dysfunctional relationships with their mothers. Many display a passive-aggressive personality, which they developed as a coping strategy because they feel/felt dominated by a female. This strategy continues to be effective in manipulating women of all ages.

D.   "I always check a bag..." His packing behaviors reveal his pathos.

He has beaucoup baggage...he keeps all his emotional leftovers neatly stored and packed away like prized possessions. He cherishes his pain and suffering. If you're really lucky, he'll share it with you! Masochism is his MO. He loves it more than he will ever love you.

E.   "A Little Bit Country"

Someone has always done him wrong. Abused, abandoned and betrayed projects are always the victims of some catastrophic event that they will never get over. He is almost arrogant in his positioning. No one knows the trouble he's seen. He loves an audience...bring tissues.

F.   "Here Comes The Rain"

Projects are "Cloud People." They can find something to be depressed about anytime, anywhere and are happy to take you out in the rain with them. This guy can barely get "happyish," never mind joyful! Something is always wrong. He doesn't feel well. His allergies are acting up. He ate something that didn't agree with him. The sun is in his eyes. You get the picture.

G.   "Serial Monogamy"

Although projects are not usually cheaters (they don't have the energy for it), they are stealers of your time and talents and great at giving guilt. He will never be ready to make a real relationship commitment in your time frame. He will use you up, wear you out, and let you down. He will hang on as long as you let him and promise to work on himself for days, months, even years. He will do almost anything to keep on your string… apron string. And then one day he will be gone. One thing is for sure, ladies: you are aging by the minute. Have you had enough?

So, how do we know for sure that this guy is a project? How many of these telltale signs does your guy display? Plenty? Your inner mixology should be recommending a different cocktail…you don't have to be drinking call brand spirits… put on your big girl shoes and belly up to a higher bar, girls. This guy will drown you in his sorrows!

3. "YOU'RE TOO GOOD FOR HIM."

OMG, she's moving back home!

This is the lie that queens pass down to their offspring with piety and panache. Whenever this phrase is aimed in your direction, it usually means you blew it.

Either you were not honest with someone or yourself about an important reality at the onset of the relationship, or when the truth came out, he took one look at the dowry and flew the coop. This is a perfect excuse for all the gals who are willing to become anything a guy, an employer, or a friend wants them to become in order to get the order. When the unadorned ingredients are served up on the silver platter, the real Cinderella offered in effigy, the alleged prince flies the coop with the girl's best friend and a picnic basket.

Sometimes we are truly "too good" for someone or something. We get disappointed when the warnings were dismissed and the inevitable occurred anyway. In this case, we must truly look at our self-esteem, or lack thereof, and realize that water seeks its own level. If we cannot see ourselves for the Grade A filet mignon that we truly are meant to be, lesser beings eventually realize that they are chopped meat and will never measure up to our station in life. The twain shall never be offered on the menu of dreams, so they move on and we cry in our soup. In this case, the feel better mantra is true, but the marinade must be examined. Why are you calling yourself a burger if you are really born to be steak tartare? Low self-esteem and lack of confidence are at the base of the broth. Better reexamine your worth, girlfriend. You can measure up.

4.   "IT'S THE LEAST HE CAN DO."

He is taking two twenties for a forty.

This is the entitlement lie of the century. Really? Anyone who truly believes that a man's sole purpose in this world is to shower you with gifts and everything your heart desires in exchange for a life sentence of abject love, poverty, subservience, and servitude is nuts. If you are fortunate enough to have a man who believes your hype, being grateful and demonstrative of your undying appreciation for his generosity and loyalty is the least *you* can do. None of us are worth the effort if a relationship is not reciprocally enjoyed, nor love mutually embraced and respected. You may have been lucky enough to trap some sweet boy with your coquettish ways and charms and convinced him of your royal status, but sooner or later he will catch on to your selfish, undeserving ways and start looking for other pastures to graze.

Taking advantage of the people you love is a lousy way to live life. It seems to me that some self-reflection and a reality check are in order. Trust me, you are not that fabulous.

5.   "YOU LOOK GOOD FOR YOUR AGE."

I will never forget the first time I heard these fatal words pointed in my direction. I almost died. What do they mean, "I look good for my age"? I look good, period! That phrase soon followed every left-handed compliment that was offered up for my consideration. Instead of being told that I had a great figure, I was discredited and justified by adding the "for your age" part. I was now being seen as a lesser being, and anything that was once an asset was somehow devalued on the open market because my status changed by the decades.

Society has a cruel way of reminding women that they are moving rapidly through the progressive dinner in life and are getting closer and closer to feasting on our "just" desserts. We have established that women tend to lose their power in society as they age. This phrase is "code," proof positive that we are getting ready to be put in a great big doggy bag and sent out to pasture.

The insidiousness of these remarks and their malevolent intentions chips away at our self-worth and confidence, rendering us sour and depressed over time. We begin to see ourselves as overripe fruit in a lesser varietal. We accept the accusation that we have been demoted to the second shelf, buying into the crap that we are suddenly less valuable human beings and a drain on our planet's diminishing natural resources. Our very age has made us less effective at work, less desirable and beautiful, less capable, less smart, and less useful in society at large…all because we are now considered a vintage wine. Ladies, as the expression goes, "Drink no wine before its time." *We* are in our prime. Live in the present. Celebrate each day. Grab a crystal goblet, pop that cork, and take a long, lovely sip of your beauty. Now is our time!

6. "YOU HAVE A GREAT PERSONALITY AND SUCH A PRETTY FACE."

Hate to say this, but if you've been hearing that your face could launch ships it's probably because it's better to hear this than accept the vision of the tidal wave being caused by the jiggling of your thunderously approaching ample hips. This is not a compliment, girls. This is a not-so-sweet warning that you may be strapping on a feedbag instead of taking a lap around the track.

Please accept this statement for what it is—the reason you dine alone. We live in a shallow, judgmental society where a first impression will dictate your future interactions and predict your overall success or failure in society as a whole. The old "what you see is what you get" is doing you a great disservice. No matter how beautiful your face or how great your personality, you may be discarded by society if you are overweight.

REJECTION SUCKS! No amount of snacks is going to make you feel better. The pain of not fitting into the popular group or a bikini for your vacation is enough to send any girl into a food frenzy.

My mother used to say, "Not everyone is going to like you." This remark tormented me because I wanted everyone to be my friend. I could not accept that sometimes people aren't nice and didn't like me, no matter how hard I tried.

Being a sensitive child meant that my feelings were frequently hurt. Being the only daughter in an Italian family also meant food was the cure for all things sad or unpleasant. "Forget about it! Have a cupcake. You will feel better" became music to my ears, and food became my medication of choice. It served as my prescription for pain relief, hurt feelings, sadness, and rejection. Rather than work through my feelings with rational conversation—which would provide solutions for my plight, insight into my experiences, offering learning, growth, potential and the latent reasons I felt so rejected—I was offered up food remedies as a constant friend in times of woe. This resulted in developing chubby thighs, attracting more ridicule, receiving deeper rejection and the onslaught of continued self-loathing. I lived in total denial and isolation. Food became my best friend, serving as a substitute for love, compassion, and friendship. I ate to feel full because my life was empty. I ate to feel loved and to distract myself from the grim reality of my painful, lonely, misunderstood life.

7.   "YOU ARE WORTH EVERY CENT."

Have   you   looked   at   the   checkbook   lately?

There is a limit to a man's patience and generosity, especially if he is paying big bucks for the pleasure of your company and is coming up short in his receivables department. A thing of beauty may be a joy forever if, and only if, the person basking in your vision of loveliness is feeling cherished. Being a high-maintenance gal is okay as long as your pedestal remains within reach of reality and of the budget. On the other hand, being too low-maintenance and extremely independent can sometimes backfire in the relationship department. All people want to be wanted and need to be needed. A totally self-sufficient gal often forgets this and winds up flying solo. A "honey do" list works in both directions. The trick is to maintain a happy medium. Figure out what you need to be happy, and what can be fulfilled by someone else. Float the notion. Also, figure out what is necessary to make the people you love happy, and invest in that annuity. Everyone wins. Once a person becomes overextended in the credit department, their loans go bad and their relationship moves into foreclosure.

Don't fool yourself into believing that your brat behavior will be tolerated indefinitely. It won't! Self-indulgent, spoiled, entitled babes are a dime a dozen. She-devils and drama queens eventually choreograph their own dastardly demise.

8. "ONCE WE'RE MARRIED, THINGS WILL CHANGE!"

Putting a lock on it! Ask 90% of married men if their sex life changed after the vows were exchanged, and they will immediately respond, "What sex life?" It seems that most women change from love goddess to vexed vixen the minute they say "I do."

The sad truth is that many women still use sex as a bargaining chip to get what they want. Once they accomplish their goal, they have no interest in having sex, even less interest in being sexy, and not at all interested in fulfilling the physical needs and emotional desires of their partners.

Sex is not a tool to achieve an end result. Accept an incredible orgasm, or two, or three. Sex is not a weapon to be hurled around like a detonator in a minefield ready to explode at any moment. Sex is a gorgeous expression of love, lust, and passion. It's a bacchanalian feast to embrace, explore, and enjoy.

Frequent satisfying sex is a physical need that, once met on a regular basis, produces enormous benefits to the body, mind, and soul. It is passion unleashed. Good sex is the best health prophylactic of all time. It helps prevent heart disease, lowers blood pressure, and releases endorphins to create a sense of contentment and well-being. It can be a full cardio workout or a sweet romantic encounter. Great sex also creates intimacy between partners and pleasure beyond compare. Battles have been won and lost, governments overthrown, families unified or forever torn apart because of sex. So what makes a girl ever think that a marriage, or any committed relationship, could survive without it?

Even the major TV networks are selling airtime to companies who are bringing toys mainstream. The ads are all about enhancing the female experience…really? It seems to me that they are still missing it: sex for a woman begins in her head…the rest is easy!

No matter how fantastic a relationship looks on paper, a marriage without intimacy is doomed. Resentment and frustration replace love everlasting. The rejection becomes unbearable, and the girl at the office or the gym becomes a fantasy frolic ripe for the picking. Mistrust and accusations replace love songs and sweet nothings, and pretty soon divorce papers are being served up instead of reservations for a romantic dinner for two.

9. "WITHOUT MR. RIGHT, MY LIFE IS ALL WRONG!"

I need a man to complete me.

When will the day come when women are satisfied with a well-balanced, full, and fabulous life on their own? When will we stop believing that we can only be complete if there is a man in the picture requiring us to do laundry, make meals, watch football, and sleep through their snoring? Why aren't we enough?

Understandably, we do have a nesting DNA and, quite admittedly, life does seem perfect when there is a man to share it with. Life, however, lived on our own terms without subjugating our authority to a male, has its benefits— benefits that far outweigh the quasi security derived from living in a loveless relationship.

Becoming a priority in your own life and putting yourself first is, at first, unnatural. We are born nurturers and caretakers. Discovering the joy that is available to each of us by creating our own priority list and a bucket list to boot enables women to live the life of their dreams. As independent, loving women, we have the right to become grown-up and gorgeous, living bold and unafraid. We can be fulfilled if we take ourselves seriously and still laugh out loud. Once we deal with our demons, clean out our emotional closets, and get back into the present, we are able to be the women we always wanted to be.

Although most of us would agree we would love to share our life with a partner, should the perfect prince not ride up on his steed, we can be successful, sexy, and satisfied with life all by ourselves!

10. "YOU CAN'T HAVE IT ALL!"

Yes, you can!

This lie is directly from the "joy stealers" of life. How ridiculous. Of course you can have it all! This limited thinking, guilt-ridden, penance-inspired mindset will certainly ruin your plans for a fulfilling life.

You can tell that this lie hits a nerve with me. First of all, what pathetic male paradigm created this blasphemy and doomed us mere mortals to a lesser life? Which scarcity-based Neanderthal ever dragged the first woman into the cave and said, "Here is your postage stamp-sized piece of the sky. Learn to like it and never leave the cave again." This particular lie must have come over with the *Mayflower*. It has been handed down through the generations to both men and women alike from the moment we took our first breath of rarified earthly air.

I can remember my mother and father warning me not to have too many expectations for my earthly existence, that I should only ask for my share and be satisfied with what I get, making sure to leave some for everybody else. It's sort of like the "just take one cookie from the tray" philosophy of life. Yes, we teach our kids to not be pigs, to share our toys and snacks, but we sure as heck shouldn't teach them that there isn't enough to go around. There are more than enough magic ovens in Heaven to go around, girls. There's no need to start sacrificing your share before you even get the light bulb to go on! This paradigm is created in the scarcity mentality—there is not enough for everyone; each of us must choose one thing to be good at, one thing that we want, one thing that we need. For God's sake, be grateful and guilty for whatever successes we achieve in life because we are certainly not worthy of any happiness at all.

The scarcity paradigm suggests that there is not enough love, happiness, and success for everyone. You better not ask for too much but, instead, like what you get and spend the rest of your life feeling guilty for whatever blessings you are fortunate enough to receive. And, never ask for another blessed thing. This is BS! When beautiful, bright, articulate women are told from early on that we cannot be fully actualized beings, we immediately are set at the buffet of life with one hand tied behind our backs and the other stuck in the strap of our very restrictive highchair.

As long as you are willing to know yourself without sauces and accoutrements, ask for what you want in life, work toward the manifestation of all your goals and dreams, and live in constant gratitude for their actualization, the world really can become your oyster, and you can lick the luscious ganache out of each and every bite.

The opposite of this bread and water scarcity model for existence is the bountiful model that says there is plenty to go around—all the love, the health, the success, the happiness that you can imagine. If you are willing to make the commitment to stay in the loving and have the courage to manifest all of your dreams into reality, then, my dears, you have permission to have it all. Shame on them, and shame on us, for taking so damn long to figure out that this is just another oppressive smoke screen preventing our clear channel shot at our life.

Now, don't get me wrong. Everyone has to make choices, and everyone has to make compromises in life. It takes a tremendous amount of faith in yourself and the universe, a tremendous amount of discipline, focus and trust, a lot of stamina, samplings, bib changes, an occasional diet, and some dessert table free-for-alls, but you will have your cake and eat it too. Just believe. You have a seat reserved at the elixir bar of life. I don't know about you, but I for one am ready to sit at the adults' table. I have my glass raised and my napkin on my lap. Bon Appétit.

Chapter 4

WHAT KIND OF COCKTAIL ARE YOU?

1. If I were a cocktail, I'd best be described as:
   a. A glass of French Champagne, a California Chardonnay, a Pinot Noir or other varietal or Bottled Water
   b. A Bourbon straight up or with a twist of some kind
   , perhaps a Beer, or a Diet Coke
   c. A frozen Margarita or other "umbrella" drink with or without spirits
   d. A Martini served straight up or a Bloody Mary

2. If I were a sandwich, I'd be:
   a. A tuna sandwich on white toast, crusts trimmed or a vegan wrap, no dressing
   b. An Italian sub
   c. A PB&J with a side of marshmallow fluff
   d. A French dip, of course

3. My favorite dessert is:
   a. Sorbet
   b. Forget the dessert, I'll have another shot! And maybe a Lolly Pop later.
   c. A fudge brownie a la mode with hot fudge, whipped cream, and a cherry.
   d. A nice, fluffy soufflé

4. My favorite fruit is:
      a. An apple
      b. A banana
      c. A peach
      d. A cherry

5. I am most comfortable dining at:
      a. An intimate, small, expensive restaurant or room service on a bad day
      b. A chain restaurant
      c. An all-you-can-eat buffet, an all-night diner, or anywhere someone else will   pick up the check because I forgot my wallet.
      d. Anywhere I am being treated royally

  The Results:
  A Champagne Girl answered all or mostly *a*'s.

  A Bourbon Girl answered all or mostly *b*'s.

  A Margarita Girl answered all or mostly *c*'s.

  A Martini Girl answered all or mostly *d*'s.

Occasionally there will be a tie. You answered an equal number in two categories. Read all about both of the girls. Take the best ingredients and make a new cocktail!

Your Cocktail Personality Revealed

The Champagne Girl

The Myth

Since infancy, you have been taught to believe that you have been divinely created better than every other girl on the planet. It's not your fault. You are simply supremely blessed! Being perfect is a tough job. The pièce de résistance has its benefits, but it comes with a hefty price tag. Your life is one of quiet desperation. Just know that the tightrope you walk creates a perfect balance for everyone in your life—except you. It's your station. "Any guy would be lucky to have you! You are the caviar on the toast points of life."

The price to be paid for your undying love and attention may be exorbitant, but you are worth every penny. Once you snag the perfectly appointed guy who will provide you with everything you need, want, and desire, one of two personalities emerge:

You will begin to manifest as a saint and dedicate your life to service, penance, and designer purses, or you can stop the pretty please behavior and become a bitch on wheels. Either way, you lose your soul. He is still the luckiest SOB on the planet, and if he lies, cheats, or leaves, he is screwed. Only death will allow him to leave the planet with his privates and dignity intact.

The Legend

Amazingly enough, Champagne Girls, your intrinsic value, come-hither glance, and bird's-eye view of the world conveys a superiority illusion pervading every socioeconomic strata and cultural background. Your apparent blessings may actually be karmic. Although Champagne Girls come from every cultural background (each with its own cultural overlay), they are most prevalent in the WASPY (the affect/attitude, not the religion or culture) conservative set.

Actually, as far as wedded bliss goes, these kinds of couples seem to put up with each other by providing the perfect foils for their reprehensible behavior. They sign up for the American Meal Plan and fully ascribe to the myth...until one day they don't. Call it midlife crisis, call it an intern, call it a drunk night on the town—once the babe/buff buns buffet is partaken, there is rarely any going back to the tuna sandwich, dry champagne, and repartee. With the European dining experience in full effect and its veritable feast of daily offerings, these love-starved people will ransom their kingdom for the opportunity to order off the à la carte menu. The breakups are what the Great American Meal is composed of, food fights and all, lest the spoils be equally divided.

The Payoff

So what is the payoff for the Holly Golightly/Mother Teresa soon-to-become Bridezilla lifestyle choice? Come on, girls, those bubbles give a girl reason to have an ample supply of gas meds on hand. There is definitely something in it for you. Why do we maintain this façade? What is the payoff?

Other people admire and respect you as a pillar of strength—the perfect wife, mother, and daughter. In addition, I will offer up a few ideas for your consideration.

First, canonization is a beautiful thing. Your daily life might be lackluster, but your reputation in eternity is brilliant. As long as you escape life with a stellar epitaph, a great portrait, and a five-star rating, being the sacrificial lamb was well worth it! Just Google yourself and see what comes up...testimonies to your attributes and selflessness abound.

Second, you wouldn't know how to live your life without responsibility anyway. So why not take a stab at it? Being the accoutrement has its merits.

Third, it's a cushy life, aka you are a tad unmotivated—okay, fearful. You could be somebody, but why bother? You are perfect just the way you are. The real world is too cruel for the likes of your gentle presence. This vaguely veiled notion that you really don't have a clue as to what to do or be in your own life mirrors your parents' dilemma when you were born. You were not a boy! You trade love and personal fulfillment for a club membership and a slew of credit cards. You possess a bottomless checkbook to prove your worth and philanthropic heart. Check out your Pinterest Boards and your Instagram snaps if you need further proof of your effervescent existence.

Fourth and finally, it's a safe bet you have read the fine

39

print on your life's "nothing sacred" contract and agreed to the terms. You will never have to do the scary work of creating your own life without a recipe. This is an equal opportunity. You offer beauty, elegance, and fill the costar role as beautiful wife and mother. Your partner offers up the cash and the dowry and the stability you crave. Your life is not about him nibbling sushi from your naked belly; it's about being old-school proper, prim, and reasonable, affording a constant diet of filet mignon, medium rare, and a baked potato loaded with low-fat sour cream. Life is perfectly predictable and wonderfully bourgeois. Unfortunately, the only passion being served up is a passion fruit sorbet.

The Spoils

A Champagne Girl remains unhappy and unfulfilled because she has become a slave to her own mythic heroine. This is the secret. You are a fraud—a perfectly manicured copy of yourself. You are a good person. You have met your parents' and your own expectations for your life.

You sang in the choir, and joined the right sorority, graduated in the top quarter of your class, majoring in art history and husbandry, and dated the class president. You got married, and now you live a perfectly wonderful life in a beautifully appointed home. You raise your kids, take

Pilates or yoga, and raise money for a children's charity.

The Cost

You have no idea who you are underneath the injections, plaques, photo ops, PTA meetings, dinners, cruises, and such. You don't have the first clue about what makes you happy because you have spent your life making others happy. You are the decorator of other people's lives. This is your station, and boy, have you been carved and served up on a silver platter for the world to eat.

But what is *your* diet? Your life is restrained, reclusive, and uninspired. Your thoughts, ideas, and passions never had a chance to manifest unless they served someone else or became a Pinterest Board.

So how can you handle the low self-esteem, transient jealousy, and gnawing insecurity you feel knowing how precariously you are posted upon your pretty perch? You really can't handle the gossip girls because you are a decent woman and don't have the coping mechanisms to become part of the Martini Club. Your kids think you're distant and strained, but the irony is that you would give anything to be hugged, truly loved, and accepted as you are. The dirty little secret? You are not perfect! It is not possible to be a beatific vision.

You spent your entire childhood trying to measure up and now that you have succeeded, you are isolated, desperately attempting to maintain the image of perfection. You know you are a fake. The pressure is too much. You know how imperfect you really are, reminding yourself every day of your many flaws.

Crushed under the weight of your tiara, you meditate and medicate…chocolate, antidepressants, Champagne. You enslave your body, abusing it daily like a drill sergeant. Your personal trainer knows you are over the edge, and so does your therapist, but they are making a good wage, and it doesn't seem like you're *that* bad off. So, you surround yourself with enablers of all kinds until one day you fall from grace. Your husband is leaving you, your kids aren't speaking to you, and your mother says you are aging faster than she is. At that point, while wallowing in a hot fudge sundae of self-pity and piousness, you have an epiphany. Why the hell am I trying to be perfect anyway? Well, isn't it time for you to discover what makes you special? And what makes you happy? And what makes you inspired? There's more to life than being the parsley on someone's plate! Discover who *you* are, what *you* like and don't like, and finally, relax. Give up perfect. Chisel yourself out of the ice sculpture. Laugh. Dance. Love. Be silly. And for God's sake, get laid!

In a moment, Heaven's gates open up. The chocolate fountain of the future starts deliciously running over, and the path to becoming a "Straight Up With A Twist Girl" rings the bell for your first happy hour. Simply, FIDO: Forget It; Dance On.

The Bourbon Girl

The Myth

You could have been a contender as a country-and-western singer, but you're just a plain-spoken girl in a one-horse town, riding bareback into the sunset. You are a tough cookie and a spirited scrapper with a six-pack and a rack in your pickup, and perhaps elsewhere.

You carry a concealed weapon and are considered one of the boys. You've been raised a bit of a tomboy and feel comfortable in a crowd. You are the brunt of a few jokes, and the instigator of a few, too. You've been raised to not be a sissy with moderate expectations and have achieved adequate results in all categories. "It is what it is" is your motto. You'll never be prom queen, but you are a star at your rodeo with your posse, and that is just fine.

The Legend

You are the most well-balanced girls at the party and see yourself with fewer layers than most. You tend to be extremely realistic about who you are, what you like and don't like, and how to get it. You accept yourself for being less than perfect and tend to be okay with espousing the attitude of "Get on my plane or get off my runway, because I am going to fly with or without you. I may not be a ten, but I am a solid six."

The Payoff

You are rarely lonely, and you have your own celebrity status among your peers. You are perceived as a great gal and are well-liked and trusted.

Your reputation for being levelheaded, cool under pressure, and loyal makes you a great mom, wife, and friend. People tend to show up at your door without notice—thank God. You love parties, so the more the merrier fits right into your daily routine. Keeping people's expectations of your abilities at a minimum, your stress level is manageable, and no one requires anything you do to be close to perfect or stellar.

You are a discount shopper and love it. Keeping people from getting too close to your inner sanctum and private life is a breeze. You entertain people on your porch or in your parlor, but rarely in a more intimate setting. At a safe distance, no one ever sees you sweat.

The Cost

Contrary to popular opinion, Bourbon Girls *do* have feelings and *do* get hurt. You may never show them, but bottling your emotions up day after day is not great for your tummy, even if it is for your jam.

You tend to be overlooked for any starring roles in life, and your nonchalant, easygoing personality tends to make guys think of you as one of them and not necessarily as girlfriend material. So you may opt to have friends with benefits, and this can lead to singing the blues...until one of them notices your fine feminine side, and then you're off to the races. They realize that you are a true, full rack of ribs with plenty of sauce, finger lickin' good!

Due to your extreme competitiveness, the boys see you as fair game, and in hunting season, they are more interested in slicing and dicing you than basting you in yummies and serving you up on their private plate. You have to know the pond you're fishing in, and ladies, you have to use the right bait if it's a kingfish you're aiming to catch. They really don't want to be in a relationship that looks more like an extreme sport than a romantic comedy. Their egos require them to remain on top in love and life.

Girlfriends are hard to come by because many women don't get you and feel inferior around you. You tend to not wear your emotions on your sleeve unless one of your posse is threatened or hurt, at which time you come out with both fists swinging and a mouth that would make a truck driver blush.

The Spoils

What do you see in the mirror? You usually underestimate your own abilities, gifts, and talents but totally ace finding a guy who loves you, eventually and forever. You raise your kids to be the real deal and manage your expectations with a look and a laugh. There are not many of you reading this book. You could care less. You are satisfied, sexy, and secure. You might even sport a tattoo.

Independent and proud to be an American, you rock! Wind up alone? You're fine with it. You are my hero! Being a

Straight Up With A Twist Girl has been your inner mixology since birth. Your strategy is sometimes one of procrastination, putting off discovering your inner passions and realizing personal goals and dreams because you are basically having a good life. Why rock the boat? Not overly concerned with appearances, aging, being prom queen, having A+ students for children, or keeping up with the Joneses, you go with the flow. Your job is over at five, which leaves plenty of time for a social life. Basically, you sail through life okay. If you ever decide to take a deeper look within yourself, you will discover a tremendous untapped resource for joy, love, and mystical transformation. If you choose to explore who you are at a deeper level, you are guaranteed to create a menu that will satisfy yourself for many lifetimes to come.

Clear and secure, uncomplicated, not too spiritual or intellectually stimulating, you are the everyday all-American upon whom our nation is built. You love your country, your kids, your lives, and your freedom. Period. You will defend your territory and your peeps. Black and white, for sure—everyone knows where you stand and what the rules are for engagement. Your plates are full and your glasses raised. BRAVO!

The Margarita Girl

The Myth

You know that you are the patient Sunday girls, the party girls, the girls who are really good people. You are honest and true blue but live behind the myth that says "as long as I'm good enough, fast enough, pretty enough, and I do anything—including give up any self-identity to make people happy—someone will love me and I will be safe. I'm not worthy of being loved on my own merits. I do not have a place in the sun unless I'm reflecting someone else's brilliance." You are the Unsinkable Molly Brown and Sabrina all wrapped up into one beautiful, scrumptious morsel.

The Legend

Everybody wants a piece of you. You are popular and you go down easy, lots to love and hard to leave…but they do over and over, with a sugar high and a satisfied sweet tooth. You are often left hearing the words, "It's not you, it's me," or "You are too perfect, you can't possibly be real. No one is this nice! You're too good to be true. I'm just not good enough for you." Sad but true, you've become a founding member of the "If I am so perfect, why am I alone?" club— not a pretty picture, but you smile anyway.

Margarita Girls tend to wear their hearts on their sleeves, along with everything else. There is no mystery to what they are thinking and feeling. Everything is right on the surface—in contrast to the Champagne Girls, who mask their emotions and thoughts with an elegant, enigmatic smile, or the Martini Girls, who will spar with you with an extra sharp instrument, sarcasm, and witty repartee. Margarita Girls are transparent and accessible but almost impossible to transform.

The Payoff

You are what all women and little girls want to be when they grow up. You are the epitome of prettiness, generosity, blessedness, and goodwill. You are low-maintenance, agreeable, affable, and available. Always. And therein lays the fly in your pie. You are admired and held in high esteem, and for this you receive plaques and accolades, compliments and gifts, love and devotion for your selflessness and dedication to always remaining true to your school.

The Cost

Because you constantly define your own happiness in the image of what other people want you to be—and therefore only exist in the reflection of someone else's image of you—you lack your own self-image and raison d'être. You have no boundaries, trading love for security, and lack self-confidence. You were patterned by your environment from birth to provide a lovely distraction for your family from their misery and stress. Your existence is also intended to decorate other people's lives. This is your life purpose as a child, and this station carries through to adulthood.

Unfortunately, as an accessory to others, you become expendable and interchangeable, assuming the role of muse, sprite, gracious entertainer, and volunteer. You feel

48

unentitled to have needs, wants, and desires of your own. You serve the people you touch. "I'm too insignificant to deserve love and to be secure by myself. I realize that I have a life and should be able to live it, but I'll give up anything to feel safe. I'll become whoever you want me to be just so that I am loved."

Making other people happy may be your forte, but you haven't a clue how to make yourself happy because no one has given you permission to do so. You are not independent, nor do you want to be. You believe that you *can* be independent but find yourself risk-adverse and resistant to change. You live in fear of being alone, possessing no palpable ego, and were taught early on to live through the superego that others have created for you. You become adept at sublimating all your own dreams, basking in other people's successes and blaming yourself for their failures. Your entire existence becomes a series of compromises, each leaving you less of a person than the one before. One thing for sure: you are HOT—a fabulously HOT MESS.

The Spoils

Let's face the facts. You have gotten your Series 7 license and spend your time selling futures of yourself on the commodities exchange. Spending way too much time buying high and selling low a piece at a time, you say, "Why am I not good enough? What's wrong with me? Why am I alone?" You undervalue your worth and underestimate your growth potential, never seeing yourself as the annuity and blue-chip stock you are truly meant to be.

You must give yourself permission to be free and find it within yourself to become your own person, satisfied and fulfilled with your own successes and living life on your own terms.

Scared to death of manifesting your own potential, you would much prefer to remain in the background and look pretty for the camera. You excel at being the wind beneath other's' wings. You are afraid of your own success and the independence that it creates. You are also scared of failure and abandonment, so basically you are just plain terrified of life in general. Lacking any experience of doing anything for yourself, you live through others without a clue of how to stand up for yourself and on your own two feet. You live your life like a great big game of Mother, May I?

The Margarita Girl's mantra is "I think I can, I think I can." Just like "*The Little Engine That Could*", you are capable of extraordinary accomplishments and feel best when your exhaustive efforts are benefitting others. Putting others' needs before your own does make you happy. You provide the very best "power assist" to anyone in need of a hand.

You are the greatest cheerleader of all! So desperate to be loved, you will do anything and become anything to be protected and directed. Unfortunately, living an entirely other-centered life leaves you open to be used over and over again in the process. Other people's opinions rule your world, and guilt and remorse become your guiding lights.

Many American women fall into this category, defining their existence and goodness by reflecting happiness in others and judging their merit by other people's opinion of them.

This becomes a roller coaster ride through a manic-depressive smorgasbord of life. You are an accessory to life, the support system, giving your own power away to your husband, children, and community. One thing is for sure: you are in constant motion. Your to-do list has no end and your phone never stops ringing. You have more invitations for parties and events than you can possibly attend. You look forward to a frozen concoction with the girls to melt your frenzy and play Ann Landers. Your nonstop life leaves no time for self-reflection. Which is just how you like it. No one would ever suspect your secret mission: distraction.

Today's reality show, survivor-centered world requires you to develop the coping skills of self-mastery and protection. Lesson one begins with "To thy own self be true."

Becoming a "Straight Up With A Twist Girl" starts with peeling back the layers, exposing your own real heart to yourself. Once you are able to reach that inner sanctum and accept the reality that no one else can make you happy, no one else can make you feel full, and no one else really cares enough to sustain you, you can start creating your own cocktail that is sweet but not sappy; strong and pure rather than frozen and fake; and clear and simple rather than cloudy and convoluted. You will become your priority, revealing how truly beautiful you can be as an independent person who chooses to live her best life as a victor, not a victim. Self-love, self-confidence, high self-esteem, independence, self-trust, and self-direction will become your inner mixology. Only then will you attract others to your life who are able to dine and drink *with* you instead of dine *on* you. You can truly begin your journey to finding real love and long lasting romance.

The Martini Girl
The Myth

Martini Madness Girls, you have issues! A great offense is your best defense. Extremely thorny and authoritative, hypercritical and high-maintenance, you share your innermost feelings with no one, and no one will ever really know you, much less love you. Not even yourself.

You are master manipulators of relationships, facts, and fiction. With impeccable timing and taste, you draw in your victims à la *Kiss of the Spider Woman*. Born dominatrices, you are always in power and always in control of every person, place, and thing that your life impacts. You never give up the reins, and you rule your kingdom with an iron fist.

So you wonder why Martini Girls spend so much of their time alone?

The Legend

Behind these women sits a little girl who is very sensitive, even shy. You were born and nurtured into becoming a painfully exacting perfectionist. The only person you're harder on than the ones you love is yourself. The Martini Girl uses sarcasm as camouflage. Being intimate with you is sort of like having a relationship with a cactus. There is probably a soothing, luscious center somewhere, but getting through the needle pricks will send most people running to the ER.

The lie this girl believes is that she has been divinely

53

appointed to be Queen of the World. Your dominion stretches way beyond your laser pointer, and as long as you have everyone at your beck and call and kissing the ground you walk on, there is peace in the kingdom...until you get bored and decide it's time to stir the soup. There is no chance that anyone will pierce the veil and see your flaws and foibles. Any of the self-adulating myths work for you. "You were born with a platinum spoon in your mouth." "That's ridiculous. Don't they know who I am?" "I'd like to thank all the little people...whoever and wherever they are..." "Just pay the man! You know I'm worth it." And yes, people do rush into service for you.

The Cost

The result of your particular worldview is that you belong to a club that no one else can join. In this place, safe and elevated, you rule your kingdom alone. Establishing and maintaining intimate relationships are not your forte. You trust no one completely.

Most people get fed up with your banter and retreat... Perfect for you. Fiercely loyal, you are always first in line to benefit from your own protection. Constantly misunderstood, you weave webs that even trap your own soul with a tangle of exaggeration, lies, and mischief in the form of schemes and dreams.

Usually one step ahead of everyone else, the drum you beat plays a solo. So Miss Martini lives a brassy, acerbic façade, both exhausted and exhausting. This façade takes a lot of work. You pretend not to care about anything or anyone, conveying the notion that nothing is worth the

54

effort. Annotating the idle life you live and the ennui you celebrate is existence's greatest reward.

This lack of motivation is a fabulous façade to hide your insecurity and angst. The reality is that you do not believe that you are actually capable of achieving anything significant, so you default to editorializing on and diminishing others' valiant efforts and search for significance. Miss Martini is a scared, insecure lass lost on her way to 'Grandma's house. The wolf costume is just a cover so that you get to choose your basket first. You tend to travel in packs, using intimidation tactics and group dynamics to control your environment. You are the "too cool for school" girls, alone and liking it that way. You are considered an egoist, perhaps even a narcissist at heart. Your favorite nickname? Bitch! You wear it proudly.

The Payoff

The payoff for you steel magnolias is that you are revered and feared, perceived as brilliant, cunning, and ruthless. You love the image. You succeed in a man's world and have been called man-eaters; you admonish all those who deny your supremacy. You hold court, fixing problems in a matter-of-fact way and demonstrating affection through "acts of service" and off-the-cuff commentaries. Your peeps get it and don't require the usual hugs and kisses, not even your children. Fixing problems is your way of showing love, even if you caused the problems yourselves. You also adore the drama they cause; the celebrity in you loves the paparazzi photo ops. They are the jalapeno peppers in the Bloody Mary of life! Delivering rapid-fire zingers, you are, quite frankly, addictive. Your peers and peeps also canonize you as the Patron Saint of the Pregnant Pause.

Immortalized by your fabulous parties and little black book of caterers, coiffures, chauffeurs and such who willingly do all the work while you take all the bows, you are a master delegator and boss. Of course, you have beaucoup free time on your manicured hands. Instead of spending it productively, you usually spend it cutting someone down to size. Somewhere there is always a stir-fry needing to be served up. Chopsticks, anyone?

The Spoils

The relationship you have with yourself can use some work. You keep pressing the pause button—a defense mechanism simultaneously protecting you from disappointment, distancing you from any potential intimacy in love, and allowing you to think that you are living a very worthwhile and fulfilling life. Okay, you could do more, but *please*, our planet is going down the tubes faster than you can say "shaken, not stirred," so why bother pitching in to save it?

So gals, you spend a lot of time on rhetoric and very little time on true love connection. You eat people for all the square meals and you are full by dessert. "Alter MY inner mixology? Are you on drugs? I was born Straight Up With A Twist. Can't handle the proof? Order a kiddie cocktail and some mini wieners. It's perfect for you! I'm on a liquid diet." The myth and unhappiness continues, making monologues an art form. You don't need anyone else. You hate competition at the mike...or the mixer.

Martini Girls have convinced themselves that the world is their oyster. And who needs hot sauce when there is a babe serving up this platter?

Chapter 5

YOU ARE WHAT YOU EAT

Fat Girls Can Rule The World

If we are what we eat, the opposite is also true: We are not what we don't eat. We are what we perceive ourselves to be. When we look in the mirror, listen to our inner circle of friends, or play movies in our head, we are what we perceive to be true. This has nothing to do with reality. We are merely a composite of all the things we have ever heard to be true about us, feared to be true about us, and experienced to be true about us. This composite picture is so warped most of the time that we cannot even begin to see any semblance of ourselves in the mirror. What we see is a montage of broken pieces and promises with a smattering of pretty smiling photos of ourselves—younger, prettier, and more naïve than we are today. Take me, for example.

I have an anorexic approach to life but am not an anorexic. It is very convenient for others to put me in that box. It gives others permission to be satisfied with their less than svelte silhouette. For me, and many other skinny girls, life is only good if I am having a "thin day." The world could be ending, I could be broke and dumped by my latest squeeze, but if I feel skinny, none of the rest matters. Feeling thin, hipbones prominent and sideways disappearing empowers me. If I feel fat, I may as well not even get out of bed; the day is doomed and everything in my world becomes a debacle. Worthiness for me is summed up on a scale. I carried my skinny mirror and my mother's scale cross-country several times because without it I could not trust myself or define my being.

One day the mirror shattered. I went into shock. Then I got up, threw out the shards without even considering using one of them on my wrists, hurled the scale into the dumpster, and took a deep breath. I became free of the reflection that enslaved me. For the first time, I was free to look at myself, and let me tell you, I was scared to death. My entire life had been consumed by my ability to govern the space I require on the planet...as little as possible. Rumor has it that a woman can never be too thin or too rich. Well, I have bought into the former and am proof positive that it's sadly purported to be true. Just ask any woman; she will adamantly agree that thinness is goddess-ness. Any woman would trade her entire net worth to be a size zero. Wow! Taking up no space becomes a religious experience.

Inside of every thin woman is a fat girl waiting to get out, and inside every fat girl is a thin woman in charge. Come on, stop threatening to throw a tantrum and hold on for just a minute. Listen to what I'm saying here. Thin women fear gaining weight more than being burned at the stake. We rule our world through an exacting series of daily calculations and tyrannically control every morsel we ingest. We balance that with an exhaustive exercise regime and excruciating guilt; all this effort in order to continue to be invisible to society. The fear of loss of control over our being and our inability to feel empowered any other place on the planet pushes us toward the brink of insanity. It's a silent I-scream sundae.

The flipside of this seemingly serene persona is the inner turmoil and unquenchable thirst to live in peace and actually be able to enjoy food without a mental calculator. We are prisoners of our own extreme self-control and our lack of control in our exterior world. The yardstick we measure ourselves against provides us a tightrope of self-loathing and occasional delight as the interior world creates our external daily experience. We do live in the present, as tortured as it is. Society adores our sprite-like bodies, as do we.

Don't get me wrong; this kind of torture is totally not worth it, unless it pays big dividends to us. And it does in the dressing room, when we discover that a size 34 or any zero or double zero fits like a charm. Or when we arrive at a luncheon or dinner, our entrance is almost poetic and the compliments abound. When we choose to speak or command a room, make no mistake, it is ours for the taking. The sad truth is that we never actually fully embrace what we look like or who we are because we can't *see* ourselves. We fear our image is constantly in a state of slipping away. The skinny girl is in negotiation with her self-worth mentally, spiritually, and physically, and some days we just want the chubby girl to win.

Our more voluptuous counterparts have the opposite life experience. Usually these gals have grounding issues and use food as a way to feel connected to the earth and their physical world. These gals use food as a conduit for staying in their bodies, and the extra poundage metaphorically insulates them and protects them from their feelings. Fat is the result of using food to offset loneliness, anger, hurt, and despair. Fries can be a fat girl's best friend.

There is nothing like a chocolate bar to make us feel loved for a few moments. But, like sex, it is short in the "coming" and long in going, going, gone.

This replacement theory adds pounds, not hugs. Fat girls are all too often shunned by society and ridiculed by every Madison Avenue talking head. Fat girls spend their lives looking for a thin dress, pushing and shoving themselves into insta-thin undies just to feel acceptable during life's most special moments.

The difference between fat girls and skinny girls is this: fat girls have developed certain coping mechanisms for the world. Most of them have a repertoire of quips and laser retorts to keep the world safely distant from their well-insulated hearts. These gals actually have power. Once they harness it and get grounded, they become the CEO of their world. This plus-size woman in charge awaits her opportunity to shine.

The skinny girl, on the other hand, is so transfixed on remaining invisible that the thought of being in charge of anything but her physical self is far removed and nebulous. Many peep over the pail and achieve great success but their own view is always in the forefront of their mind. Plus-size girls with attitude actually make peace with their booties and their souls, take residency in their fab form, and love it. These women throw caution to the wind, grab a cookie in one hand and a beverage in the other, and happily say "I'll be straight up with a twist"- Thank you.

There are cultures that admire and embrace ample women in charge and place them on a throne as they rule their kingdom. We skinnies can learn a lot about empowerment from our larger sisters. They have made peace with their girth and are perfectly comfortable in their own skin. They live in the present and demand respect. These girls are in charge, and for that, I toast them with honor. They are sexy, satisfied, and successful in their eyes.

Skinny girls tend to be a bit more concerned with the rules of engagement and others' opinions of them. The goal for us skinny girls is to relax our choke chain and enjoy life, even if it gets us into single-digit dressing. The goal for fat chicks is to get grounded, decide whether the diet is worth it, and move forward. The goal for all girls is the same. Let's raise a glass to managing "how we show up" in the world, with love and kindness. Let's get comfortable in our own skin. If we love how we look and love the world, it will love us too—at least some of it—and really, girls, who cares about the rest? There are plenty of hearts to go around. Let's start with loving our own.

Online Dating: Pre-Packaged Sex

While we are on the topic of prickly pear postures, let's talk sex.

As you might have figured out by now, I love sex. I love to make love. It'll keep you young, it'll keep you agile, and it's a much better de-stressor than a drug. My theory is all sex is good sex, as long as you are good with the terms. Terms are about you, not your partner. Terms are about what you want and what you want to get out of your endeavor in the bedroom or on the kitchen counter. Not that you need it, but let's play out a few of our all too common encounters

62

Straight Up With A Twist: Your Cocktail Personality Guide to
Finding Love & Romance

with the opposite sex in this new millennium:
Boy meets girl.

Girl is desperate to meet boy.

Boy lusts after girl.

Girl sees how much he's worth.

Girl decides she can barter her wares for happily
ever after.

Boy loves the appetizers and decides to buy the
whole enchilada.

You know the rest of the story…

Can't relate? Okay, try this:

Boy meets girl online. They lie from the get-go about who
they are, what they do, and what they want. They meet.
After the initial sticker shock, they decide to have dinner
anyway; they split the bill. They lie some more and roll
around a bit. They go through the short list of musts and
must-nots. They lie some more. They put a toe in, a foot, a
thigh, a few forced "oh my Gods," and she wakes up alone.
He just remembered he's married, changing his
relationship parameters, plus a client called. You know, a
girl can't get no satisfaction!

Happily ever after? Fat chance. The white lies, cheating,
pre-nups, post-nups, no truth in advertising, coupled with
non-communication, suburbs, carpool, late nights for

business out of town, and a case of a lot of naughty goin'
on is running rampant... Ozzie and Harriet are dead, and
so is their postwar paradigm for wedded bliss! The old
relationship model cannot exist in our new world. Casual
sex is not bringing us the desired results. The narcissistic,
indulgent, entitled twice-bitten singular sensations are
seeking immediate, no strings attached, full-frontal
immersion. Once the lust leaves, the liability comes into
focus, and we wind up alone.

We are all good at rationalizing our forays into the hay.
After we wash them out of our hair, we need to get them
off our minds, and hearts. A frisky flirt in the backseat of a
convertible with the top down makes us feel young for a
few blissful gazes into the eyes of a boy toy, and then our
knees stop working and we need to maneuver a less than
graceful exit around the gear shift. This is where we lose
traction. Most of us pretend to play a good game, but we
eventually become unhappy. We mistake a casual tête-à-
tête for a tit for tat and wind up feeling like a half-eaten bag
of white trash. Whatever happened to our glory days? They
went out of style with cocktail franks. I still love to eat 'em,
but they never taste as good the second or third time
around. I don't know about you, but in this decade I am
having a harder and harder time dealing with the heartburn
caused by fast-food piggies rolling around in my blankets.

No matter how hard we try, we cannot act like, think like,
or feel like a man. We will never experience casual sex the
way a man does because we fail to compartmentalize our
emotions. What is good for the goose is not good for the
gander. A gander cannot lay an egg. We attach. They do

not. We start fantasizing the minute we see a potential mate. We accept sex, thinking that this is what men want. At the moment, we want it too. We believe that the keys to his heart are available through intimacy. Having sex is not having a relationship. Men do not think about the future. They think about the minute. Women live through the minute, hoping it will lead to happily ever after. It rarely leads to anything other than disappointment, heartbreak, and anger.

Oftentimes we believe that we can will a man into wanting us for more than a convenient, fun encounter. The reality is that we cannot will a man to be anything more than he is at the moment we meet him. He is not, nor will he ever be, the answer to your prayers. He is interested in what he wants and does not read anything more into an evening with you. What you see is what you get with a guy. And too often, what we see is not foie gras; it's simply chopped liver. So if you can't handle the fact that your sexual encounter is what it is—and will never be anything more—then I suggest you stop trying to convince yourself and him that there is a future. There is no future in casual sex.

Self-care is in fashion in more ways than one. Care for your heart. A stand-in is not necessary for great sex. Flying solo can be very satisfying. The only committed relationship you need is the one you create with yourself. Ordering off the fixed price menu of life is predictable. No matter how much of yourself you invest in great sex and potential relationships, the results are always going to be the same: a limited menu offering quantity, not quality.

Forget your life coach; it'll only take one visit to your GYN to realize that it's a battlefield out there, and leaving with more than we came with is not a pretty picture. When the script our MDs write has more letters in it than the condition we present, we need to accept the times have been a-changing, and the alphabet soup of STDs may be longer than our last relationship.

Chapter 6

WHY DIAMONDS ARE A GIRL'S BEST FRIEND

Frenemies: Why Can't We Be Friends?

There are three reasons why diamonds are a girl's best friend. One, you can always sell them if you need the cash. Two, they require no payback when given as a token of affection, and three, it is much safer to have a relationship with the hardest substance on the planet than to trust another woman to be a real BFF! For gosh sake, you can't even trust yourself to be your own best friend. Copy?

We spend way too much time killing off the perceived "competition"—i.e., every other female on the planet except your mother and daughter. You would take out a contract on both of them at times, but let's face it, your mother got you here, and your daughter is your best bet at being sent out in the style you trained her to accustom you to. So you put up with them in the best and worst of times. Tissues and greeting cards become your mediators and your spiritual advisers, and truly, they do become your protracted lens. Every other human carrying an XX chromosome is your enemy. Trust me: somewhere, sometime, when you least expect it, even your closest friend will turn on you. She'll slice and dice you like fruit in a blender, especially if there is a man involved, and even if it's his best friend, the dog.

Let's examine the phrase, "a meal fit for a king." What happened to the queen? Is she on a diet? No, she's having her friend for lunch while noshing with the yentas at a charity cocktail party and playing cougar with the hottie behind the bar. Girls, in their present dysfunctional state, cannot be best friends. Why? Girls can never see anything in relation to something or someone other than themselves. Everything is personal—every word ever written, every song ever sang, every injustice ever committed is taken personally. It's all about me, me, me. This myopia bonds us, bares us, and blows us up. Just ask Marcia, Jan, and Cindy, the sisters who served each other up at the daily Brady brunch.

Have you ever asked for a recipe at a dinner party, the hostess agrees, conscientiously emails it to you, only for you to cook up a total flop when you try it out? Have you ever been out shopping with your BFF and tried on the dress of your dreams only to be told that it "makes you look like a house," and then see her in it the next week? How about going to a makeover and realizing the only royal treatment you're receiving is the prime spot on the gossip column's morning blog because you poured your heart out to the gal who was pouring on your mascara? Yes, this is just "between us." A girl's rendition of keeping a secret is threatening the person she told within in an inch of her life if she rats you out, and then acting horrified when your predicament is blurted out at the next philanthropic society meeting under the heading of "new business."

Girls can be loyal as long as you are all sharing the same pity party. Girls can be helpful as long as you never pass them in line. They want you to look fab only if they look a little more fab, and they want you to be in a relationship as long as they had first dibs on your guy and now the guy's considered leftovers from their party.

The competitive nature of women is warped and confused. Manipulation seems to be the only tactic on the board, and truth is just a matter of delivery and perception. There are no rules when women face off. We play to win! The spoils may be dubious, but since we can't ever believe that we can win on our own merit, we thrive on taking down any competition by extraordinary means in order to be the last girl standing. The sweeter the flavor, the bigger the bite. Women attack women in ways that men never attack men. Women cannot separate business from pleasure or our business from anyone else's—it's all their business. After all, "enough about you, it's all about me!"

Why do we perceive each other as the enemy? Did Cinderella have sisters? I rest my case. It seems that we only see ourselves having value in contrast to other women. We live in a relative world. Similes define our life experience. "I am prettier than Martha but not as beautiful as Jane." "My net worth is twice Sally's, but so is my rear end!" "I don't care. They can't even get an invitation to our club without us." "I could have had a career as a brilliant attorney, but I got married instead. By the way, that is me in that picture, isn't it?" "I really think you should let yourself go gray. Being blonde is overrated, and you're almost fifty, aren't you?" "Don't worry about your review meeting; I'll pass along your input and make your excuses. Hugs, and feel better soon!"

Wake up, girls! C'mon, really? Become the change you want to see in the world. Actually, become the friend and coworker you want to be in your world and watch what happens. It may take awhile, but once you stand your ground and embrace the women in your world with honor, we may just change our tune and return the favor, offering up the delicacy of real friendship.

Modeling auditions used to amaze me. I would walk in and there would be fifty blonde carbon copies of me sitting there. They would sneer and claw at one another like cats in heat, making eyes at the cameraman and dissing each other right and left just loud enough to get the desired reaction. Yes, fear and loathing on the work front. Then they'd prance into the audition like Pollyanna, primp and preen for the jerk behind the screen, thinking they had deep-sixed the competition and that, having seduced the director, they would be a shoo-in for the part. Pageant girls on parade, reality check! The only girl you're ever in competition with is yourself, and the only thing you accomplish by undercutting another woman is to share your seat with her in the back of the bus. STOP IT! If one woman loses her footing in this world, we all fall down.

We are here to support one another, love one another, celebrate one another, and reflect our best selves to the world—arm in arm, not toe-to-toe.

Women tend to approach the workplace like Xena the Warrior Princess. We immediately take sides, using highly developed intuitive skills, and start exhibiting pack behavior. Women never seem to mature beyond high school. It's the popular girls versus the nerds, the sweethearts versus the tough girls, the smart girls versus the smart-ass girls, and the beautiful girls versus the world. Within ten minutes of congregating, women take sides, do

the pinky swear, and defend their camp for life unless a
promotion, a problem, or a man enters the kingdom. Then
it's every girl for herself. Dispense the itching powder,
loyalty be damned!

This behavior has been the demise of women in the
workplace. We somehow feel that because it's a man's
world and we've clawed and coddled our way to the top, as
reigning queen, we won't ever let another woman close to
the throne. Women do not trust other women to be fair. The
only good coworker seems to be a maimed one.

Women cannot separate their professional relationships
from business relationships, the result being every
professional encounter is seen as a personal interaction.
Every critique, suggestion, promotion, and interpersonal
exchange is taken as a critique or a compliment about
them, not their capacity. Winning is about sweetening or
poisoning the pot. We simply do not believe, down deep,
that we are worthy of a higher position or salary based on
ability alone. If we did, we would not act so disparagingly
toward other women. If we truly believed that no one is our
competition and everyone has the right to succeed by our
side, we would bend over backwards to help one another.
Sadly, in most cases, we don't. We just pretend.

When men enter any room that women occupy, the entire
countenance changes, and these women's attention shifts
away from the other women toward the male. We suddenly
forget how smart we are and immediately default to the
ladies' room, where we check our teeth, our breath, our
lipstick, our leverage, and each other's game. We then
proceed to get the man's attention and have our way with

him, whatever our motive du jour. Period. We leave the other women at will-call, although we still believe that our girlfriends are there for backup. It's really scary and sad. We are only really significant if some guy says so…in business, at happy hour, at home, even when we are alone. We still somehow believe that we are only enough if we get the nod from the guy in the boardroom. Instead of becoming femmes d'affaires, we remain femmes fatales in pinstripe suits.

This brings me to another point. Have you ever noticed that once a girl finds a guy, she starts canceling her dates with her girlfriends, takes a powder, and never surfaces again until the relationship ends and she needs a shoulder to cry upon? This serves as further proof that women consider each other only important enough to take up the slack in life but never important enough to take precedence over your time with a man. Pathetic! I've done it too. Yes, I'm preaching to the choir on this one.

The last distasteful morsel I'd like to dish up is how women behave when men are involved in friendships. It is an absolutely bizarro world! Listen: men may turn out to be a girl's best friend. If a woman can actually establish a platonic relationship with a man, it may prove to be the most valuable investment of all time. Men are black and white. They tend to see the world in a less personal way and tend to be able to separate business from pleasure and personal agendas from professional ones. A man will usually tell you the truth unless he's sleeping with you. And a man will be loyal and realistic with you, defend your honor, explain the rulebook of the boys' club you joined, and wish you success and happiness without exception.

Men get friendship. They may be clueless in other areas, but they tend to make friends easily, keep them forever, and rarely throw each other under the bus. So what's the issue? Women don't share well. So if a man and a woman have a great friendship without intimacy and he has or gets a girlfriend or wife, there will be trouble in paradise. Women can never believe that you're "just friends." Why? Because women cannot believe that a woman can be a man's friend without benefits, other than camaraderie, companionship, and counsel.

Now, there are some areas where a platonic relationship won't cut the mustard—exes, for instance. Women do not tolerate their man having a relationship with his ex, and I think that that's just fine. It's too close for comfort, perhaps. Occasionally you will find exceptional women who can work out this built-in rub, and become friends—in which case life can become art. For most of us, it's tough. We are a work in progress. Let's start with the easier stuff.

There's lots of food for thought here. The way women treat each other is how we treat ourselves. In order to become the grown-up, gorgeous females we can be, we must take our boxing gloves off, put our kid gloves on, and have a cup of civilized tea and crumpets with each other. Establish rapport and proceed with caution in business, in friendship, and in love. The appetizer on the menu of choice must be to choose ourselves first and accept that we are valuable, worthy and deserving of joy. The second course is to choose to embrace one another and value each other as brilliant, viable, and trustworthy beings. The salad course entails assembling a network of uplifting, encouraging, and honest women and men we call friends and colleagues.

73

The main course calls for selecting a career or lifestyle that encompasses our passions and inspires our souls, challenging us to become our best and embracing us with love and compassionate relationships. The fruit and cheese course allows us to pare down our ego, keep our emotions in check, and separate reality from our delusions. Finally, dessert demands us to enjoy every morsel of ourselves and others, and always leave a little laughter for a midnight snack! Why not invite your new BFF or a guy pal over to share a piece of carrot cake, two forks and bowl of water for the pup? Leave the diamonds in the safe. He gets that it's all about you, and he's fine with it.

Why can't we be friends? Maybe it's an American thing. We were not born to be friends. From my first experience as a kindergartener, I realized two things about myself. My cubbyhole was always a mess, and most of the girls were mean and always took my stuff. The first problem was easily solved. I got a maid. The second one has been a long time resolving. Even now, when I count my friends on my fingers, I notice I have a lot of digits left over.

Women are competition for one another. We hate to lose. As a matter of fact, we refuse to lose, which provides us with a built-in passive-aggressive tendency that repels most other humans. We love to win. Unfortunately, we are not always allowed to play in the real world, and so, when we do, we make sure to take all the hostages we can, just in case we have to sacrifice a few to become the queen of the hill. No matter what sandbox we are attempting to siege, we have one thing in common: our desire to get to the top and our insecurity in believing we can ever truly get there on our own merits. If, by some miracle or sleight of hand, we do ascend to the throne, we know that it was an accident, and so we kill off any potentially significant females who might thwart our reign.

BFF IQ: Can We Talk?

So girls, if your kids start suggesting you get a dog rather than take another stab at a relationship, you know that something is wrong. A pet doesn't talk back, always thinks you're brilliant, is always happy to see you, and will die to protect your honor. They are cuddly, don't eat much, and will never tell on you. They don't care if you're broke, beautiful, or brazen.

We wonder why we would rather have a pet than a friend. So what would it take to be friends with the girls?

The Champagne Girl doesn't need friends. She prefers to drink alone. It's not that she doesn't like you; it's just that she can't trust you with her secrets. So she keeps you at arm's length, a beautifully appointed and soft distance from her heart and her journey. The only women allowed to truly befriend this gal are her mother, who taught her all she knows; her daughter, who acknowledges her flaws, keeps her secrets, and loves her anyway; and her grandmother, whose kindness and wisdom make up for the code of conduct her family required of her. That's it.

The web these girls weave is so dense that it creates the beautiful suffragette frame for her pretty, stressed face. So how does one become a Champagne Girl's friend? I have a few ideas. These girls can be found on the perimeter of the charity circuit. They usually write checks and lick postage. They serve perfect afternoon tea for monthly meetings and listen intently to the girls who circle round the teapots. You could offer to wash the dishes or clear the buffet table. Of course, they will not allow your participation. You are their guest. They will take note of your generosity and decorum and begin to observe you from a distance to see if you, too, are a member of the secret society.

Champagne Girls have a dry sense of humor and a keen sense of style, so you may find them at a trunk show for their favorite designer or a book signing for a brilliant new author. A member of her support staff, like a hairdresser, manicurist, or personal shopper, often becomes a friend by default.

So, this entrée is possible. You will be scrutinized before you will ever be asked into a dressing room to see this gal in her very expensive undies. Once you become friends with a Champagne Girl, you must pay attention to the rules of your rapport. You must never inquire about her private life, even if there is mounting evidence that something is rotten in Denmark, something like a blonde half her age. Her children and family require careful consideration, and conversation is limited to accentuating the positive in all cases. If your husbands play tennis or golf and your kids attend the same school, you have the best chance at finding a friend. Prove your worth, espouse your loyalty, and never cross the perfectly manicured lawn to peep between her shades. She will ignore you for life if you ever say an unkind word. Yours is a friendship based on mutual suffering, knowing glances, a few glasses of bubbly, a designer pre-sale, and genteel living. You must have perfect manners, speak graciously, laugh quietly, and command the shocked and slightly embarrassed glance and a knowing, enigmatic smile. In exchange for your friendship, you will always have someone to sit with who will make you proud. She will be the friend to attend events with and share the burden of raising a family and the joys of civilized living. It's a beautiful life, though perhaps a bit stuffy. Get out your pretty skirt, your starched shirt, and away you go. It's not important for her to win or brag. She knows she is the stuff that dreams are made of, even if no one else does. It's not easy to be her friend. There are lots of rules and regulations. She will always greet you with a smile, homemade cookies, and a hug.

She will listen to your woes, offer metered but sound advice, and ask for your input on certain things. She is a great friend to have, but don't expect her to get too involved in your life. It just isn't allowed.

The Margarita Girl can be most anyone's friend, at least while she's at the party. She is extremely demonstrative and can overindulge, but it's all about the fun. She lives in the present, but when the morning comes, her hangover makes her wish she could revisit the past.

This kind of girl will be in constant contact; she loves to do stuff with other girls and tends to be a bit of a gossip. She isn't mean; people just tell her their life story and occasionally she shares her wealth of information with others. So, be specific if you don't want your tale in the morning news. She can keep a secret—just remind her a time or two.

Margarita Girls are the volunteers of our society, the do-gooders of human kind. They overcommit and work their heart out by day. They spend every waking moment doing the same thing for their own family. A Margarita Girl's door is always open, her heart always available for a good cry, a hearty laugh, a confession or a pep talk. These girls make great friends. It's easy to get into the club. The dues are reasonable, the terms are flexible, but the waiting list is unbearable. She often has twenty BFFs at a time, so if you are looking for one friend for life, she may not be your girl. She rarely has time to do all the things she wants to do and is torn in all directions. She loves being the center of attention, so if you can't handle being a supporting role, she is not your kind of friend. She talks a mile a minute and lives to have fun. If you're pragmatic and plodding, she will leave you in the dust.

A Margarita Girl dresses kind of flashy—and sometimes not in the best of taste—but she can be a riot. If it's excitement you crave, her team is the one to join. She approaches her limits and freaks out when she has reached maximum capacity. Then there is usually a big confetti cannon explosion and you'll find her in tears, sweeping up the mess she made. Friendship with a Margarita Girl requires motion sickness pills because life is a roller coaster ride of highs and lows, and you never know when you'll be called on to be the designated driver. She is ridiculously loyal even when there is obvious evidence that she is being taken advantage of. She will defend you to the end and take a punch for you, too. She tends to collect people who are depressed and downtrodden, and, believe me, there is enough love to go around. Her kids are her life, her husband is her knight, and if he can't seem to stay on his horse, she'll stand by him—even if someone mentions that the horse he's trying to ride is dead. So take your vitamins, earplugs, and sunscreen. Being a Margarita Girl's friend is an amusement park ride. Just pray you love the roller coaster.

Bourbon Girls are all about ease of use. They will welcome you at their party but expect you to carry your own weight and hold your own liquor. They can't stand sissies or braggarts and hate prissies or fools. They don't mind being the brunt of a joke as long as you are game to be the target of hers. She is a straight shooter, and tact is not her strong suit. So get ready for the facts, ma'am; there's no sugarcoating of her opinions.

The good news is that she says what she means and means what she says. The bad news is that if you don't want to hear the truth, you shouldn't have asked her. This gal can be a little territorial and a tad stubborn. As long as you don't cross her and your dog doesn't use her front yard as a potty, your friendship has a chance at really existing. She loves to have fun, gets her jobs done, and doesn't mind sticking her neck out for a friend in need.

Never abuse her time or her generosity, and don't get too close to her man. You will find yourself tiptoeing through the tulips with your tail between your knees. No secondhand clothes for this secondhand rose!

The Martini Girl has only three friendship positions available: choir member, servant, or foil. Either way, you will be her audience, her stage crew or her costar, and conscience to her cause. You will have no say in any decision making and will spend a lot of time trying to mend the bridges she burns. Your opinion doesn't count, and your ideas will never be as crafty or as smart as hers. She will be hypercritical of your husband, your kids, and your car. She will direct your life like a sitcom, and you may even have to ask permission to change your hairstyle or go to the bathroom. Once this girl takes you in her fold, you will always have a part somewhere in her screenplay. Don't even think about it. You are part of her command performance team. Like it.

The first thing you must learn about befriending a Martini Girl is that you have to keep your mouth shut. She does not want to hear what you have to say, so get used to nodding and preening and mimicking her attitude and style. She will give you a mini-me makeover, and your new identity will suffice. You will spend a lot of time at her side if she deems your presence necessary, and she will expect you to drop everything and attend to her needs and whims. She demands all of your attention and will not tolerate an instant of self-reflection. Your life is all about *her*. Your importance is secondary, and so is everyone else's you know.

There can be significant benefits to being a Martini Girl's friend. You will always be a member of the cool girls club. You'll always feel and look better than everyone else. You will be treated respectfully for fear of retaliation by the queen bee herself if she catches wind that someone is messing with her friends. Her comments are scathing, but her heart is sincere underneath all that varnish. A Martini Girl can be a true friend—just keep your AA card handy.

In conclusion, a friend in need is a friend indeed.

A Champagne Girl needs a friend who maintains her composure under pressure and never asks for more than she can comfortably make available in any fashion.

A Margarita Girl needs a friend who doesn't
mind waiting on hold for her turn to speak even though she's making a 911 call.

A Bourbon Girl needs a friend who can hold her own, her liquor, and her tongue and has her back anywhere, anytime.

A Martini Girl doesn't need any friends; she needs a following. If you can provide that, she will interview you for a position.

We all need a friend who:

> Can read between the lines, see behind the masks, and laugh like there is no tomorrow and cry like the pain we see is our own.

> Is loyal when times are tough and mouths are yapping; is honest when the jaw that's flapping is our own.

> Doesn't buy our hype and could care less about our net worth.

> Can celebrate our successes and pick us up from the floor after our failures.

> Believes we are beautiful even when our behavior

has been ugly.

Will never, under any circumstances, sell us out,
sail us down the river, or trade us in for a new model.

Sees our talents and abilities and consistently
pushes us in the direction of our dreams, even if
that means we must pass them at the curb or at the
office.

Is fair in peacetime and at war, in competitions and
in politics, and does the right thing—not the popular
thing—even where you are concerned.

It's In The Bag: Your Purse Exposé

Champagne Girls always carry a chic, classic, understated
bag of medium size with a few compartments for her most
necessary accessories—lipliner and lipstick, powder (yes,
some girls still carry a compact), a matching wallet with
accompanying little black book, tissues, pillbox, and
glasses/shades. It's neat and unassuming, but don't think
for a minute it's inexpensive, sans label. You must know
what you're looking at to detect the value of this bag and
this girl. Everything has its designated place.

Margarita Girls always carry a bag that's as big as they are,
overflowing with everything, including a portable kitchen
sink. A family could live for a week off the contents of her
purse. Receipts are everywhere, wads of cash still
wrapped amid them. She has a wallet that's usually empty
except for her driver's license because she's always in a

hurry and never puts her cards back after she uses them. Then she panics and spends the day trying to figure whether there are any fraudulent charges. Her cards are discovered in the back pocket of the jeans she was wearing last night.

She's got hair ties and six lipsticks, photos of her crew, an extra clean pair of panties (just in case), cough drops and candy, gum and mints, the latest philanthropic newsletter, expired coupons and a prayer card, two pairs of sunglasses and an iPod or two. Yep, her purse has got tons of pockets and zip space, but in an attempt to be organized, she never puts the same thing in the same place twice, so her "bag life" is in a constant state of disarray, and anybody behind this chick in line can count on a half hour and a total purse dump before she finally finds a card that works.

A Bourbon Girl carries her wallet attached to her keys and her phone in her back pocket. She leaves her "overnight bag" in the car with the dogs and the window cracked. She never worries about leaving stuff in the car, because one look at her dog and no one would even think about entering. If, for some reason, she has a bag, it has one of those multi-compartment liners, and it's more organized than a church pew on Sunday morning. Her wallet is perfectly organized, too. Amazing as it is, she's a businesswoman at heart.

Martini Girls don't even carry a bag. Please. What are her peeps for anyway? They carry her stuff, answer her phone, and apply a touch-up when necessary. This girl won't even admit to wearing glasses, never mind being caught carrying them. Okay, she has a hundred purses in her closet stored by color, and when none of her peeps are available, she puts on her darkest shades, pulls out a matching accoutrement, puts a credit card, a hundred dollar bill, and a lipstick in it, and she's off. She doesn't need anything else. Her line? "Don't you know who I am?"

Happiness Comes in a Cocktail and a Cake Box

Girls, we have approached critical mass—the place where we stop bitching about our thighs and start looking through the eyes of our souls. Now that we have identified the menu offering called our life, we must take a real good look at the ingredients and then decide: is this the meal I really want to eat for the rest of my life? Is this the cocktail I want to be serving up for eternity? How will your inner mixology manifest your best life?

There are benefits and costs to baking and stirring with mixes. Some of our cakes have come out light and fluffy, and some have been used as doorstops. The handycam need not focus on the bloopers we've starred in and the mini-series we love to hate. Let's zoom in on our Botox- and filler-laden brows. The furrows tell tales that we dare not admit even to ourselves. Our lives cost us. We might as well like the batter we're lickin'.

The question is: What do we want? What kind of cake tickles our taste buds? Do we dare bake our cake without using a mix? Can we give up those umbrella drinks and become pure spirits in our very own Straight Up With A Twist kind of worlds?

Let's consider changing our recipes for the high altitude we now occupy. How can we see ourselves independent of reflection? How can we see ourselves without others holding our mirrors and prescribing our gaze? Who is the Martini Girl stripped of her repartee and her icy beverage? Who is the Margarita Girl without becoming everyone else's hot fudge and whipped cream? What does the Bourbon Girl do if there's no one to play darts with and there are no boys to chat up at the local pub? What does the Champagne Girl do if the club is closed and the martyrdom crème brûlée cracks in her designer kitchen? How can we create our own dining experience? Ladies, knocking on Heaven's door involves leaving Hell's kitchen. This is the shortcut—not short ribs recipe—for finding happiness, true love, long lasting romance and living your best life.

We have control over our lives. We do have a choice to be who we were born to be and what we choose to become. We do not have to keep ordering the same thing. We can augment our recipes for finding happiness. We do not have to maintain the paradigm we have created thus far. We can change. We can be empowered. The real question becomes, do we really want to become our best selves? Can we create an identity that allows us to be the gardener, the chef, the sommelier, and the diner of our own divine buffet? The answer is yes, and no.

We can have it all. But we must give up a lot of what we have to get what we want.

As we have discovered, there are benefits, costs, and a certain level of comfort associated with sticking to the menu we have created for our lives. There is a payoff. As long as the payoff exceeds the price we pay for admission, we will not change. In other words, unless we are truly motivated to shed our current personas and admit that we want to become our best selves, we will not change. Unless we have the courage to become the best rendition of ourselves, and the stamina to keep eating raw foods, our dreams will not come true. We must be willing to give up the alleged benefits of our current lives first and forever. We must be willing to create a new, daring recipe for fulfillment. We must learn to please ourselves.

Relationships? Let's begin by agreeing that all men are not jerks. All women are not innocent bystanders. All men are male. It is totally delusional to continue to believe we are blameless in a relationship gone wrong. We almost always refuse to see the obvious signals that men give us. We refuse to hear what they are saying loud and clear. If it is not what we want to hear, we drown them out. If you believe all of what you see and even half of what you hear, you might get the hint. He is not buying into your blueprint for his future. Denial is a destructive force. Just because you see what you want to see does not mean he is the least bit interested in sharing your vision. Get over it. Get on with it. Get out of this masochistic mess. The notion that partners complete each other makes for great tweets but authentic relationships do not complete us, which infers that we lack something, shifting responsibility to the other. Committed partners accept each other's authentic selves in our strengths and weaknesses. A contemporary authentic relationship today requires two independent and self-empowered people to choose to share the joys, the sorrows, and the responsibilities of a partnership, all the while maintaining their individual identities in a healthy and vibrant condition.

There are way too many distractions out there to go unnoticed. Once a couple commits to being a couple, they must be share a vision for each other and goals for a lifetime of real life partnership. They must also protect their relationship from social media intrusion by creating a virtual boundary, a moat around their castle.

Many years ago, Andy Warhol predicted that in the future, everyone will be world famous for 15 minutes. Thanks to social media, our fifteen minutes is now. Our absolute addiction to broadcasting every detail of our lives in posts and countless selfies supports the self-involved, attention deprived, mythic hero in each of us. We measure value in "likes" and followers and maintain our status as if our lives depend upon it…and sadly, for many it does. The older I get, the more brilliant Andy becomes. He made the ordinary, extraordinary and so do we. Boundaries are broken; people are exposed. Bullies prey on vulnerable souls and hide behind their avatars. Jealous exes seek revenge and partners spy on each other. Social sites account for more breakups than marriages. The temptation to look up old lovers, snoop into other people's private lives, and sabotage relationships is almost irresistible. And the ability to create ourselves as a pseudo "celebrity" brand is just too tempting to ignore. We have become voyeurs.

I suggest we stop watching and start living out loud.

While we're on the subject of hallucinations, I'd like to discuss another ridiculous notion—our children have become currency. Ladies, our children are not responsible for our happiness. They are not POW's in our divorce negotiations. They are not ransom, pawns, or weapons of revenge. They did not ask to be here.

They cannot save our marriage or our soul. They are not here to support us. Raise them right.

Why are you such a basket case? Some of it came from your own upbringing; generational dysfunction is a phenomena. If you really want your kids to love you, try being a parent. You are not your kid's girlfriend, sponsor, or judge. Their most important role model is *you*. If something is wrong, I suggest you take out your mirror and check in with the boss of you. You have goofed.

Carpe diem, girls. You are all you have. You might as well serve up something you are proud of baking and even happier to be eating. If this is your last supper, why have fast food? We have created codependent relationships with our entire inner sanctum. Time to make the donuts!

Our peeps will be appalled at our process and may even go into a starvation mode just to see how determined and committed we are to changing our world. It's all going to hit the fan. Our world will rock. Count on it. Our friends and lovers, children, and even our pets, will go on a hunger strike. They will pick out their food, spit it out onto a napkin, go on a starvation diet, and curse the day you ever picked up this book. But ladies, I promise you, you are worth it.

Champagne Girls have a reverent following that relies upon selfless acts of service to survive. The local charity you've been supporting may not like the fact that they will have to replace you with two paid employees or a novitiate saint, but they'll find someone to wear your angel wings. Lingerie stores can only use so many models. Giving up the joy of baking two hundred cupcakes for the annual bake sale with your right hand and setting a pristine table with your left is tough. You may no longer receive handwritten thank-you notes from the kindergarten class or accolades from the husbands whose wives entertain with paper plates, but you will make room for creating your own menu. You may actually get some sleep. With a bit of time on your manicured hands, you might find time to play the piano, or take a class. Make house keys for your kids and a reservation for dinner with the boss and his wife. Carve out time to dabble in the fine art of your self-creation.

The Margarita Girls may have to miss a few parties, but trust me: the music will play on ad infinitum. Promise yourself that whenever you get an invitation for happy hour, it's your happiness you're imbibing. There are more lost souls on the planet than novenas for you to murmur. Tell them to get a therapist, because this girl is into self-celebration—hold the salt and the lemonade. You are all about designing your own ice cream topping and drizzling it all over prospects that will relish licking your spoon.

Martini Girls may be the hardest converts of all. It's really hard to replace an audience as well-heeled as yours. It's almost tragic to think about all the perfectly paired repartees falling upon lesser ears. Who will do your dirty work and prep your kitchen? Well, ladies, it's time to roll up your sleeves and realize that sous-chefs are expendable, but your soul is not. Take off your stainless steel corset and python stilettos and get naked. Your peeps will cry as you ceremoniously disrobe. Your dominatrix tendencies will fall away, and your softer side will emerge as chiffonade and meringue. You may be surprised that your peeps will shed a tear. They may need to slap each other a time or two. My guess is they will stay by your side and become the taste testers in your newly embraceable, unfettered miracle whip kitchen.

Bourbon Girls just need to step up their game with an infusion of confidence and motivation. Stop relying on takeout menus and precooked meals. Mediocre may be okay for an occasional feeding frenzy, but you owe it to yourself to become a Julia Child's Coq au vin! You'll become a bit difficult, complicated, and persnickety, perhaps, but you are capable of birthing a gorgeous golden egg. Just accept the fact that you are a tad lazy in the self-actualization department and a touch overzealous in the bar games and gang warfare. And for God's sake, stop cleaning off everyone else's plate. You were not born to become a human vacuum. You are too territorial. Annex a new kingdom—your personal dessert domain.

When we decide to go on an organic diet and stop ingesting crap, everyone is forced to change their diet and shake off those extra pounds. As my BFF says, "self-preservation is a ?!?!?! and I'd rather be ?!?!? than get !?!?!" Yes, it's a sad tale, but embrace it. You are not a lobster. Get out of the boiling water and bask in the sunshine of your own love. Who are we at the organic level? What is our passion?

And do we have the courage to raise a glass to toast our convictions? Here is the recipe for becoming your own master chef:

1) Be realistic about the life you've baked and the cocktail you are presently serving. Acknowledge and accept responsibility for your fallen soufflés.

2) Discover your unique palate. Design a balance of salty, sweet, savory, and piquant taste sensations. Create a cocktail that truly is divine to the last drop. Experiment with new recipes for happiness.

3) Make a list of *your* necessary life ingredients. What are your priorities? What are the non-negotiable in your life and relationships? Where can you compromise and still emerge victorious?

4) Prioritize your spending. Create a budget and categorize your calorie investments as well as your financial balance sheet. What will it take to be independent that doesn't involve a name change?

5) Stock your pantry with nourishing foods. Limit those luscious libations to a manageable amount…take

6) heed if you are sipping yours out of a sippy cup, dearies….Cut out the
crap and make a plan for your success.

7) Refurnish your kitchen with fully functioning machinery that creates opportunities for change.

Throw the rest out. Get rid of everyone and everything that keeps you in your old belief system.

8) Forget the blender. Chop your own veggies; mash your own bananas and the mint for your mojitos. Cooking is an exquisite exercise, a free-form art, and a Zen moment. Don't cheat yourself out of experiencing and ingesting the lessons only small detail work reveals. Do your homework. Get disciplined and start moving. Look at your own two hands. Start kneading your way to the top.

9) Join a cookie co-op or create a happy hour empowerment pack and share your newly baked self-creations with other self-actualizing chefs. Find a new group of friends who align with your goals and dreams.

10) Replace your mother's cookbooks and cocktails. Live on your own terms. Accept the blame you would prefer to assign elsewhere. We learn more from our failures than we ever do from our successes.

11) Invite dinner guests who will be satiated and stimulated by your fine dining experience. Choose to interact with people who want what you want and who think you are fabulous. There are no free lunches.

12) Take off your apron, say a blessing, taste a bite. Linger, smile, raise a glass, and say, "I choose to

be neither shaken nor stirred. Here's to being Straight Up
With A Twist."

Champagne Girls, Margarita Girls, Bourbon Girls, and
Martini Girls—stand up and be counted! Skinny girls,
chubby chicks, babes in the woods, and vintage selects—
unite! We are on the verge of greatness. The only thing
standing between you and a degree from Le Cordon Bleu
is your willingness to be a standalone delicacy and your
desire to order your own drinks and pay for your own meals.

Embrace one another, stand up for one another, and learn
to love yourselves. I believe you were born to do this. So
what do you say?

Chapter 7

LIFE WITHOUT DOGGIE BAGS, CONTAINERS AND PLASTIC WRAP: YOUR EMOTIONAL RESCUE

Enough with the leftovers. Who are you saving them for? Life is about living in the present, not about lugging all those debunked leftovers that have been in the fridge for days, months, and years with you for a midmorning snack. Containers and plastic wrap may provide a hermetically sealed time capsule for your past behaviors and indulgences, but let's face it: that menu didn't meet your culinary expectations the first time, and it certainly won't serve you well now. The past is over, and the only thing that you accomplish by hanging onto it is the extra calories you packed on when you ate it the first time.

Women love to be emotional pack rats. We love to take out our miseries and reexamine them under a microscope, embellish our memories, cherish our heartaches, and linger on every last self-righteous breath. With all the new fangled gadgets on the market , we are certainly not alone in our quest to preserve our memories. The difference between great ones and rotten ones are that the good ones taste better the following day, and then they're gone. The trouble with our emotionally toxic leftovers is that they never disappear. They rot somewhere in the recesses of our mind and fester. Once discovered, they give off a noxious odor and become lethal. Still, we reseal them and keep them for another day.

Personally, I believe that doggie bags are a waste. I don't

94

have a dog and can't stand anything reheated or lukewarm. Life without a doggie bag embodies the "Straight Up With A Twist "philosophy. You won't starve—the children in Biafra aren't getting them—and the initial dining experience, if you were truly present, was totally satisfying.

Eat in the present tense. Enjoy each sensory-filled moment—the texture, the aroma, the taste, the appearance, and the company—even if it's just you. And when you're full, be happy and be done. There is no need to pick the bones clean another day. Mindless eating and pounding those cocktails down is like distracted sex. Why bother? Eating while on the computer, watching a movie, or driving is like trying to have an orgasm with a football game on—someone may be coming, but it's not you. Enjoy now. Be present. Your presence is the gift you give yourself. Open it up and take a big, juicy bite!

On to the stuff in the plastic containers. Why do we savor our unresolved karma?

Two reasons. First, it further invests us in our self-defeating image and reaffirms our station in life, thus making us secure, even in our misery. Our baggage helps define who we think we are. It has become part of us and is deeply rooted in our childhood experience and the coping strategies we adopted for survival. Life without baggage frees us to become what we want to be. That is, if we dare to live without the boundaries that our baggage creates. Karma proves our existence and encourages us to play out our personality as our menu selection. It's safe. We know who we are by the type of baggage we carry, and so does everyone else.

Second, there is a payoff in this emotional triage. We are getting something out of it—an audience, attention, pity, a check—something that makes us feel worthy. Leftovers continue to feed our egos, allowing us to remain right, justified in our vindictiveness, resentment, and pain. Unresolved emotional issues grow mold and poison us, even if they are neatly packaged in the latest fashion color container. Vengeance, bitterness, and hatefulness are reserved for powers higher than a girl in six-inch heels. We reap what we sow. So if you think that super gluing your ex's keepsake china together or meticulously slicing and dicing his Italian custom-made suits is going to get you brownie points in Heaven or any satisfaction, you might as well put on the well known anthem and take a powder.

If it's true that our face tells our life story, your face is going to start looking like the protagonist of a sci-fi novella, baby, because you are becoming one really scary chick. Revenge is not your life's work. There is no such thing as getting even. Kick those emotions to the curb. They will consume you. Stop spending your time plotting someone else's demise and start investing in your own toxic cleanse. Bottoms up.

So listen, have a party. Invite your peeps. Spend an evening looking at each other's emotional leftovers, commiserate, cry, laugh, get angry, vent. Turn on the garbage disposal of life and throw them down the drain. Grind up all your old negative thoughts and feelings. Let them go. Rinse the sink with forgiveness and self-compassion, and finally, move on.

Life without leftovers is a revolutionary

concept. Dare to eat fresh food every day. Dare to be present. Dare to redefine yourself. Forget being a pack rat. Give up the crap. Choose joy. Fill your containers with leftovers of love if you want, or recycle them. Remember, food has an expiration date, and so should your baggage. When it no longer serves you, get rid of it. FIDO...Forget It; Dance On.

Chapter 8

DIM SUM OR DIM WIT: IS YOUR MAN A PROSPECT OR A PROJECT?

Let's not forget the guys. They have baggage, too—no one gets away unscathed. Their Tupperware is full of only two kinds of leftovers, though. First, financial, financial, and financial, and second, unresolved girl-done-me-wrong feelings. Eighty percent of men hold hostility over unresolved financial transactions, usually involving a certain kind of settlement punctuated by monthly payments and a mediator. Anyone who has dated a recently or not-so-recently divorced inductee into the school of "you cannot believe what that bitch did to me!" will find these fellows to be very upfront about their recent trip to the cleaners and their determination of never going there again. All affairs of the "heart" are directly tied to his net worth—or the recent lack thereof—and all of his venting and indignation stems from this leftover disbelief and aggression. The emotional baggage is directly in proportion to how much it cost him to get out of it or how much it hurts him in the pocketbook. Yes, man has two brains. One is fixated on sex, the other on money. And when they work in consort, the domino effect can be brutal.

The twenty percent of men who actually have heart baggage become life members of the bubble boy club. They resolve to become impermeable and insulated. They take their heart off their sleeves and sanctimoniously place what's left of it in Tupperware, sealed tight, vowing never to let a woman taste the sweet vulnerability of this boy again.

With enough prodding, he may divulge the harrowing tale of the woman who broke his heart, resplendent with a guitar solo and a twang. He may even shed a tear, but the one thing he will never do is open up and commit to another female again.

Depending upon where you encounter this guy along his road to becoming the emotional iceman, he will present himself in different ways. Early on in the leftover process, he will be raw with the emotions of despair and depression, perfect for a Margarita Girl dressed as Florence Nightingale. He will fill up every corner of your compassionate heart and cry on your shoulder for as long as you let him—days, months, and yes, my girls, even years. Once the scab has fallen away and the scar over his heart has formed, he'll kiss you gently, thank you for the rest of his life, cock his head, and bid you a fond farewell. Later in the process, his affect is recognizable by his sincere boyish smile, sort of shy but infectious distance, and a polite and proper demeanor. He'll take you out for a while, be a gentleman and scholar, and then one day he will simply vanish.

So here is the deal, gals. It's all about your choice. The thing about baggage is this: it'll be there until you throw it out. And once you discard your own leftovers, your option is simple. Do you really want to take on someone else's plastic containers and call them your own? Do you really want to dine on someone's half-eaten sandwich for the rest of your life? It's your choice. Guy A will require a long and arduous pre-nup, your signature on a "collision damage waiver," and constant reassurance that you are not there to take whatever is left of his money or his ego. He'll never truly trust you, and you will have to be able to pay your bills on an ongoing basis. Life with this guy is a negotiation, and it does get old, like yesterday's baguette. Stale and sophomoric, sooner or later you are going to want to hit him over the head with it. Guy B is a project, not a prospect. Get your tissues and your blood pressure meds ready. It's gonna take a lot of both, and he will never come around, at least not in your time frame. You will end up alone, I promise: worn out, done in, older and blue. Which brings me to our next subject, playing your options.

Life is like a Chinese menu. It's impossible to read, there's a lot on it, none of it is good for you, and after awhile, no matter what you choose, it all kind of tastes the same.

Well, this is your former life. Welcome to the à la carte menu.

Choice is a powerful thing. Whether you want to or not, you are making choices every minute of your life. And the crazy thing about not choosing is that by not making a choice, you are making one anyway, so you might as well choose. My method, one from Column A and one from Column B, allows the maximum taste sensation, and the great thing is that you are never locked into the same meal twice. Empowered women have the ability to choose their menu in life and in love. It's all about weighing your options and remaining flexible. It's calisthenics on a cake plate. Commit to strengthening your core, and all options become possible. The combo plate can be different every day depending upon your whim. Imagine eating dessert first!

I offer you a new paradigm for living: the options menu.
This is how it works. First, let's suspend your not-so-
rational life credo up until now. Let's go way back in time,
before the invasion of the voices in your head. You
remember, when you lived in your own paradigm of loving.
What if we could create a relationship based on love
instead of fear? How would it look? Let's imagine:

First, we must let go of fear. What would it take to live
unafraid? Wow, I remember unafraid.

I felt safe and secure for my future.

I liked me.

I was so excited to be me and to discover how wonderfully

I was made.

I would take risks.

I would laugh a lot.

I would play.

I would have shelter.

I would have enough food.

I would have value—young or old, skinny

or fat, smart or silly.

I would be loved for who I am, not for who I am expected to be.

I would be honest with myself. Lying is very fattening. Anesthesia wears off.

Champagne gets expensive, as does a sashay down the racks at our favorite store.

Delusion becomes asphyxiating.

I would be one with truth. Truth would dictate my decisions based upon the highest and greatest good for me first.

I would eat me whole. Imagine, life without leftovers.

I would be courageous and live out loud.

I would remain in the loving, not in the loathing.

I would be empowered, passionate, and present.

I would acknowledge my feelings and respond, not react, to disturbances in the spirit field. The knowingness that directs my life comes from my authentic self.

I would be okay by myself. Scratch that. I'd be brilliant by myself!

I would be proactive, doing what and who pleased me.

I would not fall victim to the neurotic layers of voices screaming ice cream, caviar, toys, and Bad Boys.

I would honor the essential me who whispers joy, love, constancy, beauty, passion, care, independence, and freedom.

I would live life reverent and aware of my inner child.

I would be innocent and live out loud.

I would be me.

So how does this sound? Once we can imagine what life might be like singular, sensational, and self-satisfied, we can then move into what we want. We actually have a shot at eating dessert first and loving it. If I can achieve autonomy, truly love myself, and just believe that I am the pièce de résistance of my life, I will become a Straight Up With A Twist Girl and always be manifesting the best of my inner mixology.

So, let's recap. What does it take to be free?

1.   Become who you always wanted to be. Create your own recipe for living. Save for the raw ingredients—your talents and dreams—discard the other ones. It's amazing how many times we agree to eat things that we don't really like because it seems easier than making our own creation.

2.   List the qualities you love about yourself. Choose to celebrate and honor those gifts every day.

3.   Accept who you are today in the present. There is no past and no future. Accept that everything that you

have experienced until now has been a projection or a memory. You're a creation in the making. The best bread takes awhile to rise and requires special handling.

4. Dare to become self-sufficient. Yes. It is time to become responsible for our lives, our choices, and our bills. Face it and then grace it. Reorganize, readjust, realign, and readdress while recycling the rest.

5. Get rid of the impostor versions of you. Focus on your truth. You've wasted enough calories on fake food.

6. Base your decisions on what suits you – not your boss, or your kids or your BFF.

7. Do not fall into default. Deny fear!

8. Choose love, and start loving you.

Chapter 9

How To Bed A Bad Boy Without Being Burned!

In our search for real love and long lasting romance, we encounter all kinds of men along the way. Each of them has their charms. Each of them reveals something about ourselves that we need to learn. There are innocent first loves, projects, prospects, and then, there are Bad Boys, the most dangerous males on the planet.

The Bad Boys can do more damage to a woman's heart than getting trampled by the tidal wave of shoppers stampeding through the department store doors on Black Friday.

Yes, with all the field research and rug burn marks I've received while foraying into the dark side of loving Bad Boys, you might say that I have a doctorate in this addiction! And yes, girls, let's call it what it is: an ADDICTION!! What is it about our absolute inability to resist their lusty come-hither glance? They are eye candy for the soul. And how about their ever so well-rehearsed casual repartee? It's music to our ears. And they're all too well coifed and appointed bodies and scent de jour? It's sweet elixir for the girls who want to be hypnotized and swept away by the baddest boys on the planet. Gigolo? Romeo? George? Peter? The names may change but the game is the same. The essential skill set that they share is the ease with which they will bring you to your knees in the heat of passion, cause you to hear the angels sing in the throes of love making, whisper sweet nothings (emphasis on NOTHINGS) into your ears...leave you breathless...and then neglect to call you back...ever again! And you knew it from the minute you locked glances. Oh, the shame of it all!

Champagne Girls love the fact they know better than to be seduced by the likes of them. And yet, no man has ever made them feel so alive and utterly female. The Bad Boys love ingénues...forbidden fruit. The Margarita Girls stand in line for a shot at one night in their powerful arms. Somehow they believe that being on the arm or between the sheets with these guys is going to boost their sadly lacking self-esteem. Delusional! The Bad Boys devour them like appetizers and then move on to the Martini Girls for their main course. Martini Girls are their only suitable opponent in strategy, love and lust. They neither play by the same rules and become, nor take, prisoners. Unless, of course, its handcuffs... The Challenge of bedding a

Martini Girl provides the ultimate rush for a Bad Boy. They love the game and actually play it better than they do! They respect the heck out of this dominatrix' and often are secretly intimidated by their power. The mutual attraction and fierce frolic burns white-hot and usually explodes...but why not? Where else can they find this kind of entertainment? On cable? LOL! Bourbon Girls rarely fall for them but every once in a while they have to experience the hypnotic and hyper real life of free falling into the arms of the devil! No matter what our cocktail personality, we drink the potion every time and beg for more. Let's get one thing straight: These guys are not real love and long lasting romance candidates! Still ready to romance and dance with them? OK. Me too.

How do you stay in the game without an intervention? There are rules! I have decided to share my Bad Boy survival guide with you...because we choose to bed them...so let's thrive, girls! Admitting we have a problem is the first step!

The truth about Bad Boys is that they are all little boys who had their heart broken badly by some girl and have vowed never to let it happen again! All women are accessories. They make no commitments. They only love themselves. They trust no one, not even their mother! As a matter of fact, their childhood may very well be where this whole thing started. Imagine that? Being a victim of their childhood? Tsk tsk. Aren't we all?

How do you bed a Bad Boy without getting burned? You learn how to decipher their secret language and decode their lie. You become an expert on bringing them to their knees. Dress the part. Rehearse your lines. And become a master at the fine art of blowing them one last kiss.

1. ADMIT YOUR ADDICTION: Hi, my name is... and I love Bad Boys. To know them is to love them. Accept the bare facts, girls: we are card-carrying members, we crave them, we fantasize about them, we salivate over them and we will not stop! Let's call it what it is—we are simply addicted to the dark side and have decided they are worth it. No analysis needed. They are the twist in our cocktails du jour...tsk tsk.

2. HAVE AN EXIT STRATEGY IN PLACE: Begin with the end in mind. We all know how the story ends, ladies. Ride Darwin's draft: Survival of the fittest is key. Plan your survival by firmly establishing your break point and vow to go no further. These boys all use the same playbook. You know the flow of this liaison. What is your last straw? Resist the temptation to slurp...this tall cold one is not good till the last drop. You pre-decide when you have had enough...and commit to leaving with your dignity intact.

3. WEAR PROTECTION! Using condoms never allows you the opportunity to be completely vulnerable to these guys. That is what they want! They want to know that they have put their narcissistic stamp on you forever...that they purchased your total net worth in bed! Standing up for yourself and insisting on condom use will drive them crazy. At first, it will add another level of excitement for them. Your ability to protect yourself gives them reason to keep coming back for more! They love a challenge and getting you to have sex without protection will be their goal. Once they accomplish this—it is usually "game over." Using condoms not only protects you physically by providing a boundary. It provides you with distance. Condoms give you a layer of emotional protection as well. You are one layer removed from being "totally in." Condoms give a girl a sense of independence that Bad Boys crave and admire. Girls who love Bad Boys need to remain in charge of their bodies, minds, and souls.

4. "DARLING SAVE THE LAST DANCE FOR ME." Do not allow yourself to become emotionally attached to these boys. Keep your dance card full and occasionally let that fact slip. Having other men wine and dine you while you're dating these boys will create a barrier for your emotions that will keep your heart protected, your mind distracted, and your availability low. BTW—Bad Boys love the competition…you'll soon be treated like a queen…they can't stand to lose.

5. NEVER LET THEM SEE YOU SWEAT! Needy Girls need not apply! Do not ask questions about the past, the present, or the future. Live in the moment. Don't ask anything that would require them to lie or puff their egos up more than necessary. You don't care what they do when they are not with you and you could care less about anyone else they have on a leash. This requires discipline, girls. Do not start fantasizing about "happily ever after" with this dark knight." That is not the horse you're riding. Remain emotionally aloof but totally engaging. The less you say, the more they will want to know why you don't seem to care about their antics! Competition? What competition?

6. KEEP THEM GUESSING—BE MYSTERIOUS! Tell them nothing about your past. Give them little insight into what you are thinking and less insight into how you are feeling about him. Self-disclosure is a taproot into your vulnerability. Silence is golden! Bad Boys need to be the center of attention. Keep your eyes in flirt mode but your mouth shut. For him,

it's all about the chase and the fantasy of your fabulousness. They will become consumed with you. PERFECT!

7. DEVELOP REPARTEE! Bad Boys love smart, sassy women. Become a conversationalist with game.

   Have an opinion and voice it. Bad Boys respect the heck out of any woman who can hold their own in a man's world!

8. SHOW APPRECIATION! Yes, these guys need to know that you appreciate every morsel of their highly cultivated personas! Compliment them. Thank them. Show that you adore them but DO NOT worship them or you will be downgraded to groupie status.

9. SEX IS AN EXTREME SPORT—DIVE IN! Bad Boys are usually great in bed. My God, they should be—they have certainly had enough practice!!! And yes, they consider their expertise extraordinary in all the world and want to impress you with their know-how and abilities! FAB FOR YOU! They also are skilled in the art of seduction and love the pas de deux, so, by all means, let them do the dance! After all, that is precisely why we love them!! Bad Boys will be absolutely floored to discover that you, too, are highly skilled in the art of seduction and sex. They will be in bliss. As long as you can handle the action, they will desperately desire to keep you in

the dance…and even after, you will play on in their memory as the best dessert ever…mmm, good!

10. BLOW THEM ONE LAST KISS! Always be the one to leave the liaison first. Bad Boys will be done with you sooner or later. Empowerment for women begins with knowing when they are about to move on from you and beating them at their own game. No matter how hard this is…you MUST bid them farewell first. It will keep your dignity intact and give you a sense of empowerment. It will also maintain their respect for you and yes, keep their ego in check. They will never get over the fact that you dashed—TTFN, boys!

HOW TO BRING BAD BOYS TO THEIR KNEES.

Follow the above rules to a tee!

TELL TALE SIGNS: Their fall from grace:

1. Your dates move from weeknights to weekends. Imagine that?

2. You receive calls and texts at random times during the day just to say "Hey!" He's wondering what you are doing and with whom. Be elusive and do not always be available.

3. He plans your evenings in advance. They are getting more special by the minute.

4. PDA! Only when a Bad Boy is truly interested in you does he show affection in public, especially around his friends. I'm not talking about lewd and lascivious here—real intimacy…a whisper, a private joke, holding hands.

5. He tips his hand by letting you in on his fascination with you.

6. He CASUALLY asks you about your current relationship status, past lovers, and other strangers. DO NOT TAKE THE BAIT!

DECODING THE LIES: Four in Hand

THE ART OF OMISSION

Bad Boys don't feel the need to lie. They are comfortable with their myopic world view, incorrigible behavior, and narcissistic ways. Bad Boys have convinced themselves that they are the most honest men on the planet because they rarely will make up and share a complete untruth. They have handlers for those details.

Commission is not necessary once you have mastered the art of omission. There are two types of lies. Commission is the art of fabricating tall tales. Omission is the art of leaving out certain important information to lead your heart down the desired path of belief. It's the old adage: ignorance is bliss. These guys simply leave out any details that would cause a girl to feel badly about herself, or him.

They are brilliant at creating smokescreens that distract women from learning the juicy details of their secret lies. They have more plots than a novelist. They didn't lie to you. They simply omitted to tell you the whole truth. Vagueness is their Black Leather Jacket Coat of Arms.

SELF-DISCLOSURE

Bad Boys will "confidentially" disclose to you intimate details of their "back story." These thoughts, deeds, and relationship stories are shared to make you feel like "you are the only one." Sorry, gals—this soliloquy is fully rehearsed. Believe me, you are not the first, the last, or the only one to hear this crap. Listening to gut-wrenching stories about their past and watching them get all teary-eyed is a ploy used to gain your trust and access to your heart and panties. They need you to believe that down deep, they are good people. They must have that validation on a regular basis. Their conscience is not clear. I'll buy the popcorn, you bring the tissues. These are award-winning performances.

EVERY ONE LOVES A PARADE

Hate to say it, girls, but you will be paraded around like a homecoming queen on a three-scoop float. He is a creature of habit and the two things he can't avoid are: feeding his veracious appetite for adoration by showing his world that he has made another successful trip to the babe buffet. And realizing how thinly veiled his seduction routine really becomes when he offers the EXACT same dining experience to every single girl he desires to eat. A Bad Boy truly feels that he is much too clever to ever be caught in the "You are the only woman I have ever brought here, done this
with, etc." One look at the maître 'd's eyes will give him away.

SERIAL MONOGAMY

Guys who have perfected this lie are very clever and extra dangerous. Over time and at a certain age, the veteran BBs and the early inductees share an inability to keep multiple babes in the air at one time. They develop the concept of serial monogamy, which is shorthand for "I am too lazy, too old, or too tired to keep more than one girl on the hook at a time. So I will be with you exclusively until I

114

tire of you." Because we think in terms of "happy ever after,"
we get sucked into believing that the Bad Boy you're
bedding has changed; he has had an epiphany. You are
really the one who converted him from his life of sin and
debauchery. TAKE A POWDER, GIRLS!!! BAD BOYS
NEVER CONVERT!!! Refer to Rule # 10. Some of them
just run out of steam!

DRESSING THE PART:

Bourbon Girls don't have to dress the part. They are not
interested in bedding these boys. They have a slew of Bad
Boy friends who think they look mighty fine for being a girl!
You command the room in those tight jeans, tailored shirt,
and a hint of cleavage provided for their viewing pleasure.

Margarita Girls provide a never-ending main course for
these guys; they will have you for breakfast, lunch, and
dinner. You provide the perfect foil for their machismo. You
are vulnerable, needy, easily impressed and always seem
to be hanging around in the right places. Sexy and a little
trashy is the way to get these guys to come over. Dressing
a bit like a cherry tart will ensure that he licks your plate
clean.

Champagne Girls will only fall for Bad Boys when they are
desperately sad and vulnerable. Bad Boys love
Champagne Girls because bedding one is like receiving a
pay raise. They just moved up the social ladder, feathering
their nest and flattering their ego. They can fantasize night
and day about slipping off the lace and slipping on the
satin sheets. The more demure and doe-like your glances,

the more refined, soft, and conservative your demeanor, the more wolf-like his advances.

Martini Girls and Bad Boys have too much in common to ever be a match made in Heaven. Although they respect the heck out of each other's game, and enjoy sumptuous meals and fabulous forays in the hay, the bottom line is that Martini Girls do not sufficiently feed a Bad Boy's ego. They are perfect matches in intellect, wit, humor, sex, and gaming. One or the other will cry uncle when the handcuffs get too tight in their black leather boudoir. Both of them need an audience. Both of them require their partners to become indentured servants and neither of them are willing to give up the reins...so wear whatever you want, Martini Girls. You are a vixen, they know it and love letting you on top for a while. They will absolutely strap on the helmet, hop on the back of your bike and smile while you take them on a very memorable ride!

Enough said.

Chapter 10

HAVING DESSERT FIRST: IF MARIE ANTOINETTE RULED THE WORLD

Give the girl a break. She was only fourteen when she became the Dauphine of France, then the world's largest empire. Marie Antoinette was set up at birth to be used as collateral. She married the lame duck, Louis XVI, and, being a Margarita Girl, she did exactly what she was supposed to do. She attended to her kingly project with reverence and decorum. Although she loved champagne, she was not constrained by her station in life. She partied with princes and paupers and bedded soldiers, and vetted her share of Cruellas with cause. She propagated and promulgated and celebrated her birthday with panache and irreverence. She delighted in watching the sunrise, wearing exquisite shades of pink taffeta and devouring royally iced petit fours. She lived out loud as a Straight Up With A Twist Girl with poise. She even created her own grounded home where she could raise her children as she saw fit, with a bourgeois peace of mind, not so far away from the facades espoused by her nobility.

She was unafraid and impetuous. She embodied all the qualities that we need to be—fearless, untamed, self-aware, realistic—and was a social activist in her own right. She kept a keen eye on personal liability and honor, but her power was usurped, and so she defaulted to denial. Unfortunately, her rebellious spirit was contorted and crushed under the weight of the throne. Her powerlessness to have any input as to her 'country's authority or her sovereignty was thwarted. Uneducated in these matters, her reputation suffered, and she became the brunt of her subjects' ire and frustration. When France collapsed at the hands of its own enablers and fops, she merely offered up her favorite menu choice, and for this they beheaded her.

Typical. And we think we have it bad. She may have chosen to "let them eat cake," but I will add "cut me a corner piece while you are at it." Her plan could have worked, if she was only allowed to rule her kingdom and take charge of her life. But no, off to the guillotine went she. The sad fate of this Margarita Girl makes one weak in the knees.

In our recent history, a most lovely Champagne Girl emerges, Audrey Hepburn. All little Champagne girls need a grown up Champagne Girl for a role model...and sometimes we need more than one because the lessons they teach are rarely spoken. They are inferred. My mother was a Champagne Girl and her grace under fire transformed my worldview and shaped my soft little being into a discerning and acquiescent young lady. She was extremely private-almost reclusive to others but to her family she had limitless love, patience and accessibility.

As a Champagne Girl in training, I studied my lessons well and tried to emulate my mom in many ways. In my kindergarten class for Halloween I was given an orange box and told to ask for pennies for the poor children who had no food, nor shelter from the harshness of life. A picture of Audrey Hepburn holding a sick and dying child so touched my heart that from that day forward, I wanted to become just like her too, a woman of service and compassion, and my mother- a woman of great style and discernment. I am here to share that sometimes dreams really do come true... maybe not exactly as you picture them but in retrospect, life will unfold exactly as it is meant to be if you choose to follow your dreams even though the road is long and winding.

One day I received a letter saying that Miss Hepburn was coming to South Florida and asking me to co-chair an event in her honor. By that time, I had retired from my career, and living the life of a mother, wife and child advocate in our community. It was and was not the life that I had imagined but as a Champagne Girl, I did my best and tried to make a difference for the children in our town who needed shelter from a violent life. At 31 years old, in a small Italianate foyer in a very grand home I met my role model-face to face, hand in hand, just the two of us in a moment where there was no time and space. There was just love, deep respect and appreciation among Champagne Girls. We immediately recognized each other as such. That is a moment that I shall never forget.

Miss Hepburn was a true Champagne Girl. She lived her public life with great clarity and compassion. Her words were well chosen, metered and handsomely delivered. Her beauty and grace were undeniably pedigreed and her fortitude and resilience spoke volumes. I had the great honor of standing by her side the very next evening as she greeted a crowd of eager fans and supporters –each with a story, a check and a camera. Miss Hepburn was quite sick at that time and although I thought her energy must have waned and pain level was unbearably high, she stood and greeted each and every one of the 500

119

guests who waited patiently to meet this iconic humanitarian, academy award winning actress, mother and friend. Miss Hepburn looked extraordinary in her chignon, her soulful eyes dressed with liquid liner, and her simple and elegant dress. To a Champagne Girl, subtraction is sublime and Miss Hepburn needed no accessories to enhance her brilliance. From Sabrina to Eliza, Breakfast at Tiffany's to Charade she brought to life the very essence of what it is to be a true Champagne Girl and immortalized every moment of the persona for us to enjoy and embrace forever. Her filmography is an encyclopedia and homage to the spirit of this Straight Up With a Twist personality. Her private life remained private. Her public life needs no further explanation. She was a penultimate Champagne Girl. There will never be another Audrey…we were all blessed to have the one and only.

Only Catherine the Great could represent a true Martini Girl. I mean, after all, only a truly great Russian leader can exemplify and truly be appreciated as a vodka martini. Of course they attributed her death to a sexual encounter with a horse—a girl with a libido, what a concept! Catherine was a woman's woman in a man's world. She had her posse. Several, as a matter of fact. She annexed countries and company with a single gaze, controlled her people with a certain benevolent tyranny, and was the patroness and grand architect of a new dawn in her homeland. She surrounded herself with confidantes and counselors who paid undying homage to her intelligence, zeal, and unilateral governing style. Her repartee was the acid test, and many lesser intellects wound up exiled or otherwise excommunicated from favor. She led her country and herself with courage and bravery, living on her terms with many romances, involvements and forays into uncharted waters. ' This girl had her priorities straight and a game plan in mind whenever she danced a pas de deux. She loved and left them on her terms, creating her own mythology. She wore her crown valiantly and ruled with an iron fist and a velvet glove, which she might have had several uses for... but that's a horse of a different color. Long live Catherine, our emancipated Martini Girl! Like her or not, she was a mover and a shaker. See what you could become if you became your highest self? It's "Noblesse Oblige" with attitude. You could rule the world and still have time to get into something more comfortable before dinner. Bottoms up!

Okay, so Elizabeth I got off to a rough start. The illegitimate child of Anne Boleyn and King Henry the Eighth, she witnessed her mother's beheading as a child, setting her sights clear for life. Self-preservation is all about negotiating the terms of engagement. She mastered this, and so should you. Do you notice a trend developing between certain death and utter emancipation? I guess we have made a few advances in the past five hundred years—not many, mind you, but that one is a plus.

Elizabeth lived in obscurity and obfuscation, learning survival skills early in life. Becoming "one of the boys" but enjoying many of the benefits to being a girl paid off for Liz in the long run. Being a very practical girl, she adopted one of her mother's mottoes, *video et taceo* ("I see, and say nothing"). This strategy, viewed with impatience by her counselors, often saved her from political mistakes and marital misalliances. A savvy horsewoman and archer, she rarely missed her target. Prudent and slow to react but decisive in her rule, she was England's answer to a Jack Daniel's Girl in charge. A realist, practical and unwavering, this girl was a survivor. An expert in creating allies with men, she had a special way of leveling the playing field, which allowed her to rule with a certain common charm and erudite nature. She invented the pancake makeup approach to fashion and became a superb actress, a charismatic ability that all Jack

Daniel's Girls share. This fab imagining allowed her to live two lives, side by side, a public and a private one. This ability to step in and out of character is a lesson all Jack Daniel's Girls should learn and a behavior they should master. This woman of two bodies, one mind, allows this often perceived tomboy to enjoy the rather softer side of the female without giving up market share of control over her public domain.

This practical queen was often noted for fulfilling her duties and doing things right, a true Jack Daniel's Girl trait. If something is not done right, it is not worth doing. So, my Jack Daniel's Girls in training, what do you think? Imagine if you could rule your world with the decisiveness, self-knowledge, utter security, and esteem of Queen Elizabeth I. You too, might have your cake, and eat it, too.

The lesson here is simple. Throughout history, there is evidence of great women accomplishing great things within the paradigm created by contemporary society. We have the opportunity to bake our cake and eat it, too. Marie Antoinette, Jackie, Catherine, and Elizabeth are just a few examples of truly actualized women of their time. They could not live beyond the paradigm of their station, because the world was a very different place in those days. They could, however, find freedom and independence in thought and action within the confines of the court they addressed.

We are the jury and judge. All too often we do not give ourselves our fair day in court. We plea bargain away our chance at self-fulfillment and success by believing the excuses we create within our personalities. Stop taking and making excuses for your lack of self-actualization. They do not serve you. We only have one shot at this fabulous life buffet. Let's not live it shaken and stirred. Take a bite. Make a toast. Celebrate your inner mixology. I dare you. C'mon, just try it. Become a Straight Up With A Twist Girl and never be mistaken for a call brand again!

"I am not afraid...I was born to do this." Joan of Arc

Chapter 11

BLOW ME ONE LAST KISS

Congratulations to all of you who have digested every morsel of this book and celebrate your inner mixology. You realize what kind of cocktail you're serving and have become intimately aware of the attributes and tribulations of your brand. It's time to create your own recipe for having dessert first, setting your life—not your kitchen—on fire!! Whether you crave a Champagne Girl's soufflé or a Margarita Girl's flambé—you are taking the challenge of becoming the woman you have always wanted to be when you grew up...a girl who embodies the Martini Girl's wit, the Bourbon Girl's grit, a Champagne Girl's pedigree, and a Margarita Girl's coquetry. Yes, happiness does come in a cocktail and a cake box. And yes, you can redecorate or remix it every day by taking the best of each of the Girls and incorporating them into your core. Live a little! Taste them all! Your BFF posse must have all the girls present to rule the bar and your hybrid personality blend can serve you best, straight or on the rocks, whenever the need arises. You are finally an empowered woman who can size up any happy hour situation, pivot on her well-appointed heels at a moment's notice, smile and say, "Blow me one last kiss."

How do you find real love and long lasting romance? As this book has revealed, you must first fall in love with yourself. Create a relationship with yourself that honors your authentic inner mixology. Once you understand your cocktail personality, transform yourself from living a

"Shaken and Stirred" existence to an empowered life, and accept who you are as a woman worthy of happiness, love, and prosperity, you will be able to clearly begin to envision the man of your dreams. Manifest someone who will meet you at least half way and share your tastes and recipes for living your best lives as partners, friends, and lovers.

In closing, this is the whole point, girls:

I do not care how you show up...I do not mind who you are. Actually, I love who you are. I love you enough to tell you the truth. The only thing I care about is at the end of the day when you look in the mirror you like what you see... no, that you love what you see. No, that you are passionately in love with you woman you see.

Beyond the insecurities and false eyelashes, tight jeans and toxic glances, deafening negative self talk and silent longings, bitchy retorts and quiet tears, deeply know that you are enough and that this one precious life is waiting for you at then end of your façade. The only person who can give you your life is you.

Whether you find the love of your life or not doesn't really matter. It would be fantastic if your do... but you may not. Whether you become all that you thought you could be in the "real" world is really irrelevant. What other people say or think about your life and your choices will not make you fulfilled. Collecting stuff and convincing yourself that it's going to make you happy is a lie. Investing time and energy in the hopes of finding someone who will bail you out of the mess you have gotten yourself into is most likely NOT going to happen. What matters most is that you take charge of your self, your behavior, your thoughts, your feelings and your body. Fight every day to create a life that you deserve. You have the right to be happy. You have the right to be successful. You have the right to be independent. You have the right to be loved. You have the responsibility to do it by yourself and for yourself.

You have the tools and wisdom to be independent. You have the opportunity to create relationships that matter. You do not have control of all the experiences that you encounter but you do have control, over how you reframe these experiences into life lessons and live your life to the highest and best use of your unique gifts talents and voice.

You are alone regardless of your relationship status. We are all alone on our journey here. We can walk side-by-side, arm in arm with love and compassion and courage. We can witness each other's lives and celebrate each other's beauty, we can fight the good fights and we can laugh until we cry. I suggest you do, with all your heart and every once of your might. That is what it means to live your life "Straight Up With a Twist."

Leave your excuses on the floor. They no longer serve you. We have paid the price for our freedom its time to start investing in our future in this world and in the next. Collect experiences that become your story. Tell your story and create a legacy within the hearts of those you love. Leave a soft footprint on the beautiful world that is uniquely yours in service to another. It does not matter that you are immortalized. Really. Trust me, we are and are not, that special. What matters is that you have lived and that the work continues…the work of being an infinite soul having

126

a gorgeous loving human experience.

I urge you to step up and become more than your façade.
They are so overrated. I love you. That's a start. The rest,
is up to you.

About Mary

Mary Giuseffi is a former Ford Model, Relationship Expert, Personal Brand Consultant and Social Diva who knows how to create a spicy and authentic life. You have seen her most recent TV appearances on the Today Show among others, sharing her wit and wisdom on how to live your best life and create successful, long lasting relationships.

Mary works around the world with successful and aspiring entrepreneurs, authors, and real people who are ready to live the life of their dreams. Her clients have been seen on the Today Show, Good Moring America, Oprah, Dr. Oz, America's Biggest Loser-the list goes on and on... She spreads joy and inspires success for those who seek happiness and prosperity.

Mary is passionate about all things "children", has been a mentor, volunteer and activist on their behalf for decades. She worked with Audrey Hepburn for UNICEF, her very own dream come true and has received many accolades for her philanthropic endeavors. In 2014, she received the distinguished honor of being among Broward County's 100 Most Outstanding Women.

Mary spends her time Florida, NYC and LA and when she is not there, you will find is traversing the globe as a single, sassy, self-made, bon vivant whose glass is always full regardless of the pour.

CPSIA information can be obtained at www.ICGtesting.com
Printed in the USA
LVOW07s0802220815

451155LV00032B/1142/P